Andrew Dickson White

The Warfare of Science

Andrew Dickson White

The Warfare of Science

ISBN/EAN: 9783743305441

Manufactured in Europe, USA, Canada, Australia, Japa

Cover: Foto ©ninafisch / pixelio.de

Manufactured and distributed by brebook publishing software (www.brebook.com)

Andrew Dickson White

The Warfare of Science

THE

WARFARE OF SCIENCE.

BY

ANDREW DICKSON WHITE, LL. D.,

PRESIDENT OF CORNELL UNIVERSITY.

NEW YORK:
D. APPLETON AND COMPANY,
1888.

ENTERED, according to Act of Congress, in the year 1876,
By D. APPLETON & CO.,
In the Office of the Librarian of Congress, at Washington.

TO

HENRY WILLIAMS SAGE,

OF BROOKLYN, N. Y.,

A CHRISTIAN MAN, WHO HAS PROVED THAT HE WELCOMES ALL TRUTH, AND FEARS NONE,

THIS LITTLE BOOK IS INSCRIBED,

WITH FEELINGS OF

THOROUGH RESPECT AND ESTEEM.

PREFATORY NOTE.

In its earlier abridged form this address was given as a Phi Beta Kappa oration at Brown University, and, as a lecture, at New York, Boston, New Haven, Ann Arbor, and elsewhere. In that form, substantially, it was published in THE POPULAR SCIENCE MONTHLY. I have now given it careful revision, correcting some errors, and extending it largely by presenting new facts and developing various points of interest in the general discussion. Among the subjects added or rewrought are: in Astronomy, the struggle of Galileo and the retreat of the Church after its victory; in Chemistry and Physics, the compromise between Science and Theology made by Thomas Aquinas, and the unfortunate route taken by Science in consequence; in Anatomy and Medicine, the earlier growth of ecclesiastical distrust of these sciences; in Scientific Education, the dealings of various European universities with scientific studies; in Political and Social Science, a more complete statement of the opposition of the Church, on Scriptural grounds, to the taking of interest for money; and, in the conclusion, a more careful summing up. If I have seemed to encumber the text with notes, it has been in the intention to leave no important assertion unsupported; and in the hope that others —less engrossed with administrative care than myself—may find in them indications for more extended studies in various parts of the struggle which I have but sketched.

A. D. W.

CORNELL UNIVERSITY, *March*, 1876.

THE WARFARE OF SCIENCE.

I PURPOSE to present an outline of the great, sacred struggle for the liberty of science—a struggle which has lasted for so many centuries, and which yet continues. A hard contest it has been; a war waged longer, with battles fiercer, with sieges more persistent, with strategy more shrewd than in any of the comparatively transient warfare of Cæsar or Napoleon or Moltke.

I shall ask you to go with me through some of the most protracted sieges, and over some of the hardest-fought battle-fields of this war. We will look well at the combatants; we will listen to the battle-cries; we will note the strategy of leaders, the cut and thrust of champions, the weight of missiles, the temper of weapons; we will look also at the truces and treaties, and note the delusive impotency of all compromises in which the warriors for scientific truth have consented to receive direction or bias from the best of men uninspired by the scientific spirit, or unfamiliar with scientific methods.

My thesis, which, by an historical study of this warfare, I expect to develop, is the following: *In all modern history, interference with science in the supposed interest of religion, no matter how conscientious such interference may have been, has resulted in the direst evils both to religion and to science—and invariably. And, on the other hand, all untrammeled scientific investigation, no matter how dangerous to religion some of its stages may have seemed, for the time, to be, has invariably resulted in the highest good of religion and of science.* I say "invariably." I mean exactly that. It is a rule to which history shows not one exception.

It would seem, logically, that this statement cannot be gainsaid. God's truths must agree, whether discovered by looking within upon the soul, or without upon the world. A truth written upon the human heart to-day, in its full play of emotions or passions, cannot be at any real variance even with a truth written upon a fossil whose poor life ebbed forth millions of years ago.

This being so, it would also seem a truth irrefragable, that the search for each of these kinds of truth must be followed out on its own lines, by its own methods, to its own results, without any interference from investigators on other lines, or by other methods. And it would also seem logical to work on in absolute confidence that whatever, at any moment, may seem to be the relative positions of the two different bands of workers, they must at last come together, for Truth is one.

But logic is not history. History is full of interferences which have cost the earth dear. Strangest of all, some of the direst of them have been made by the best of men, actuated by the purest motives, and seeking the noblest results. These interferences, and the struggle against them, make up the warfare of science.

One statement more, to clear the ground. You will not understand me at all to say that religion has done nothing for science. It has done much for it. The work of Christianity has been mighty indeed. Through these two thousand years, despite the waste of its energies on all the things its Blessed Founder most earnestly condemned—on fetich and subtlety and war and pomp—it has undermined servitude, mitigated tyranny, given hope to the hopeless, comfort to the afflicted, light to the blind, bread to the starving, joy to the dying, and this work continues. And its work for science, too, has been great. It has fostered science often. Nay, it has nourished that feeling of self-sacrifice for human good, which has nerved some of the bravest men for these battles.

Unfortunately, a devoted army of good men

started centuries ago with the idea that independent scientific investigation is unsafe—that theology must intervene to superintend its methods, and the Biblical record, as an historical compendium and scientific treatise, be taken as a standard to determine its results. So began this great modern war.

GEOGRAPHY.

The first typical battle-field to which I would refer is that of Geography—the simplest elementary doctrine of the earth's shape and surface.

Among the legacies of thought left by the ancient world to the modern, were certain ideas of the rotundity of the earth. These ideas were vague; they were mixed with absurdities; but they were *germ ideas*, and, after the barbarian storm which ushered in the modern world had begun to clear away, these germ ideas began to bud and bloom in the minds of a few thinking men, and these men hazarded the suggestion that the earth is round—is a globe.[1]

---

[1] Most fruitful among these were those given by Plato in the *Timæus*. See, also, Grote on Plato's doctrine of the rotundity of the earth. Also *Sir G. C. Lewis's Astronomy of the Ancients*, London, 1862, chap. iii., sec. i. and note. Cicero's mention of the antipodes and reference to the passage in the *Timæus* are even more remarkable than the original, in that they much more clearly foreshadow the modern doctrine. See *Academic Questions*, li., xxxix. Also, *Tusc. Quest.*, i., xxviii., and v., xxiv.

GEOGRAPHY.

The greatest and most earnest men of the time took fright at once. To them, the idea of the earth's rotundity seemed fraught with dangers to Scripture: by which, of course, they meant *their interpretation* of Scripture.

Among the first who took up arms against the new thinkers was Eusebius. He endeavored to turn off these ideas by bringing science into contempt, and by making the innovators understand that he and the fathers of the Church despised all such inquiries. Speaking of the innovations in physical science, he said: "It is not through ignorance of the things admired by them, but through contempt of their useless labor, that we think little of these matters, turning our souls to better things." [1]

Lactantius asserted the ideas of those studying astronomy to be "mad and senseless." [2]

[1] See *Eusebius, Præp. Ev.*, xv., 61.
[2] See *Lactantius, Inst.*, l., iii., chap. 8. Also, citations in *Whewell, Hist. Induct. Sciences*, Lond., 1857, vol. i., p. 194. To understand the embarrassment thus caused to scientific men at a later period, see *Letter of Agricola to Joachimus Vadianus* in 1514. Agricola asks Vadianus to give his views regarding the antipodes, saying that he himself does not know what to do, between the Fathers on one side and learned men of modern times on the other. On the other hand, for the embarrassment caused to the Church by this mistaken zeal of the Fathers, see Kepler's references and Fromund's replies; also *De Morgan, Paradoxes*, p. 58. Kepler appears to have taken great delight in throwing the views of Lactantius into the teeth of his adversaries.

But the attempt to "flank" the little phalanx of thinkers did not succeed, of course. Even such men as Lactantius and Eusebius cannot pooh-pooh down a new scientific idea. The little band of thinkers went on, and the doctrine of the rotundity of the earth naturally led to the consideration of the tenants of the earth's surface, and another germ idea was warmed into life—the idea of the existence of the antipodes, the idea of the existence of countries and men on the hemisphere opposite to ours.[1]

At this the war-spirit waxed hot. Those great and good men determined to fight. To all of them such doctrines seemed dangerous; to most of them they seemed damnable. St. Basil and St. Ambrose[2] were tolerant enough to allow that a man might be saved who believed the earth to be round, and inhabited on its opposite sides; but the great majority of the Fathers of the Church

---

[1] *Another germ idea,* etc. See *Plato, Timæus,* 62 C., Jowett's translation, N. Y. ed. Also *Phædo,* pp. 449, *et seq.* Also *Cicero, Academic Quest.,* and *Tusc. Disput., ubi supra.* For citations and summaries, see *Whewell, Hist. Induct. Sciences,* vol. i., p. 189, and *St. Martin, Hist. de la Géog.,* Paris, 1873, p. 96. Also *Leopardi, Saggio sopra gli errori popolari degli antichi,* Firenze, 1851, chap. xii., p. 184, *et seq.*

[2] For opinion of Basil, Ambrose, and others, see *Lecky, Hist. of Rationalism in Europe,* New York, 1872, vol. i., p. 279, note. Also, *Letronne,* in *Revue des Deux Mondes,* March, 1884.

utterly denied the possibility of salvation to such misbelievers.

Lactantius asks: "... Is there any one so senseless as to believe that there are men whose footsteps are higher than their heads?—that the crops and trees grow downward?—that the rains and snow and hail fall upward toward the earth? ... But if you inquire from those who defend these marvelous fictions, why all things do not fall into that lower part of the heaven, they reply that such is the nature of things, that heavy bodies are borne toward the middle, like the spokes of a wheel; while light bodies, such as clouds, smoke, and fire, tend from the centre toward the heavens on all sides. Now, I am at loss what to say of those who, when they have once erred, steadily persevere in their folly, and defend one vain thing by another."

St. Augustine seems inclined to yield a little in regard to the rotundity of the earth, but he fights the idea that men exist on the other side of the earth, saying that "Scripture speaks of no such descendants of Adam."

But this did not avail to check the idea. What may be called the flank movement, as represented by Eusebius, had failed. The direct battle given by Lactantius, Augustine, and others, had failed; in the sixth century, therefore, the opponents of the new ideas built a great fortress and retired into that. It was well built and well braced. It was nothing less than a complete theory of the world, based upon the literal interpretation of texts of Scripture, and its author was Cosmas Indicopleustes.[1]

According to Cosmas, the earth is a parallelogram, flat, and surrounded by four great seas. At the outer edges of these seas rise immense walls closing in the whole structure. These walls support the vault of the heavens, whose edges are cemented to the walls; walls and vault shut in the earth and all the heavenly bodies. The whole of this theologic, scientific fortress was built most carefully, and, as was then thought, most scripturally.

Starting with the expression, Τὸ ἅγιον κοσμικόν, applied in the ninth chapter of Hebrews to the tabernacle in the desert, he insists, with other interpreters of his time, that it gives a key to the whole construction of the world. The universe is,

[1] For Lactantius, see *Instit.*, iii., 24, translation in the Ante-Nicene Library; also, citations in *Whewell*, i., 196, and in *St. Martin, Histoire de la Géographie*, pp. 216, 217. For St. Augustine's opinion, see the *Civ. D.*, xvi., 9, where this great Father of the Church shows that the existence of the antipodes " nulla ratione credendum est." Also, citations in *Buckle's Posthumous Works*, vol. ii., p. 645. For a notice of the views of Cosmas in connection with those of Lactantius, Augustine, St. John Chrysostom, and others, see *Schoell, Histoire de la Littérature Grecque*, vol. vii., pp. 37, *et seq.*

therefore, made on the plan of the Jewish Tabernacle—box-like and oblong.

Coming to details, he quotes those grand words of Isaiah, "It is he that sitteth upon the circle of the earth, . . . that stretcheth out the heavens like a curtain, and spreadeth them out like a tent to dwell in,"[1] and the passage in Job, which speaks of the "pillars of heaven."[2] He turns all that splendid and precious poetry into a prosaic statement, and gathers therefrom, as he thinks, treasures for science.

This vast box is then divided into two compartments, one above the other. In the first of these, men live and stars move; and it extends up to the first solid vault or firmament, where live the angels, a main part of whose business it is to push and pull the sun and planets to and fro. Next he takes the text, "Let there be a firmament in the midst of the waters, and let it divide the waters from the waters,"[3] and other texts from Genesis. To these he adds the text from the Psalms, "Praise him, ye heaven of heavens, and ye waters that be above the heavens,"[4] casts that outburst of poetry into his crucible with the other texts, and, after subjecting them to sundry peculiar processes, brings out the theory that over this first vault is a vast cistern containing the waters. He then takes the

[1] Isaiah xl. 22.
[2] Job xxvi. 11.
[3] Genesis i. 6.
[4] Psalm cxlviii. 4.

expression in Genesis regarding the "windows of heaven,"[1] and establishes a doctrine regarding the regulation of the rain, which is afterward supplemented by the doctrine that the angels not only push and pull the heavenly bodies, to light the earth, but also open and close the windows of heaven to water it.

To find the character of the surface of the earth, Cosmas studies the table of shew-bread in the Tabernacle. The dimensions of that table prove to him that the earth is flat and twice as long as broad; the four corners of the table symbolize the four seasons. To account for the movement of the sun, Cosmas suggests that at the north of the earth is a great mountain, and that, at night, the sun is carried behind this; but some of the commentators ventured to express a doubt here; they thought that the sun was pushed into a great pit at night, and was pulled out in the morning. Nothing can be more touching in its simplicity than Cosmas's closing of his great argument. He bursts forth in raptures, declaring that Moses, the prophets, evangelists, and apostles, agree to the truth of his doctrine.[2]

---

[1] Genesis vii. 11.

[2] See *Montfaucon, Collectio Nova Patrum*, Paris, 1706, vol ii., p. 188; also pp. 298, 299. The text is illustrated with engravings showing walls and solid vault (firmament), with the whole apparatus of "fountains of the great deep," "windows of heaven,"

GEOGRAPHY.   17

Such was the fortress built against human science in the sixth century, by Cosmas; and it stood. The innovators attacked it in vain. The greatest minds in the Church devoted themselves to buttressing it with new texts, and throwing out new outworks of theologic reasoning. It stood firm for two hundred years, when a bishop—Virgilius of Salzburg—asserts his belief in the existence of the antipodes.

It happened that there then stood in Germany, in the first years of the eighth century, one of the greatest and noblest of men—St. Boniface. His learning was of the best then known; in labors he was a worthy successor to the apostles; his genius for Christian work made him, unwillingly, Primate of Germany; his devotion afterward led him, willingly, to martyrdom. There sat, too, at that time, on the papal throne, a great Christian statesman— Pope Zachary. Boniface immediately declares against the revival of such a terrible heresy as the existence of the antipodes. He declares that it amounts to the declaration that there are men on

---

angels, and the mountain behind which the sun is drawn. For an imperfect reduction of one of them, see article *Maps* in *Knight's Dictionary of Mechanics*, New York, 1875. For still another theory, very droll, and thought out on similar principles, see Mungo Park, cited in *De Morgan, Paradoxes*, 309. For Cosmas's joyful summing up, see *Montfaucon, Collectio Nova Patrum*, vol. ii., p. 255.

the earth beyond the reach of the means of salvation; he attacks Virgilius; he calls on Zachary for aid; effective measures are taken, and we hear no more of Virgilius or his doctrine.

Six hundred years pass away, and in the fourteenth century two men publicly assert the doctrine. The first of these, Peter of Abano, escapes punishment by natural death; the second, known as Cecco d'Ascoli, a man of seventy years, is burned alive. Nor was that all the punishment: that great painter, Orcagna, whose terrible works you may see on the walls of the Campo Santo at Pisa, immortalized Cecco by representing him in the flames of hell.[1]

Still the idea lived and moved, and a hundred years later we find the theologian Tostatus pro-

---

[1] Virgil of Salzburg. See *Neander's History of the Christian Church*, Torrey's translation, vol. iii., p. 63. Since Bayle, there has been much loose writing about Virgil's case. See *Whewell*, p. 197; but for best choice of authorities and most careful winnowing out of conclusions, see *De Morgan*, pp. 24–26. For very full notes as to pagan and Christian advocates of doctrine of rotundity of the earth and of antipodes, and for extract from Zachary's letter, see *Migne, Patrologia*, vol. vi., p. 426, and vol. xli., p. 487. For Peter of Abano, or Apono, as he is often called, see *Tiraboschi;* also, *Ginguené*, vol. ii., p. 293; also *Naudé, Histoire des Grands hommes accusés de Magie*. For Cecco d'Ascoli, see *Montucla, Histoire des Mathématiques*, i., 528; also, *Daunou, Études Historiques*, vol. vi., p. 320. Concerning Orcagna's representation of Cecco in flames of hell, see *Renan, Averroès et l'Averroisme*, Paris, 1867, p. 328.

testing against the doctrine of the antipodes as
"unsafe." He has invented a new missile—the
following syllogism: "The apostles were commanded to go into all the world, and to preach
the gospel to every creature; they did not go to
any such part of the world as the antipodes, they
did not preach to any creatures there: *ergo*, no
antipodes exist." This is just before the time of
Columbus.

Columbus is the next warrior. The world has
heard of his battles: how the Bishop of Ceuta
worsted him in Portugal; how at the Junta of
Salamanca the theologians overwhelmed him with
quotations from the Psalms, from St. Paul, and
from St. Augustine.[1] And even after Columbus
was triumphant, and after his voyage had greatly
strengthened the theory of the earth's sphericity,
the Church, by its highest authority, was again
solemnly committed to the theory of the earth's
flatness. In 1493 Pope Alexander VI. issues a
bull laying down a line of demarkation upon the
earth as a flat disk; this line was drawn from
north to south, west of the Azores and Canary
Islands; and the Pope, in the plenitude of his
knowledge and powers, declared that all lands

[1] For Columbus before the Junta of Salamanca, see *Irving's Columbus*, Murray's edition, vol. ii., pp. 405-410. *Figuier, Savants du Moyen Age*, etc., vol. ii., p. 394, *et seq.* Also, *Humboldt, Histoire de la Géographie du Nouveau Continent*.

discovered east of this line should belong to the Portuguese, and all discovered west of it should belong to the Spaniards. This was hailed as an exercise of divinely illuminated power in the Church; but in a few years difficulties arose. The Portuguese claimed Brazil, and, of course, had no difficulty in showing that it could be reached by sailing to the east of the line, provided the sailing were sufficiently long-continued. The bull of Pope Alexander quietly passed into the catalogue of ludicrous errors.[1]

But in 1519 Science gains a crushing victory. Magalhaens makes his famous voyages. He proves the earth to be round, for his great expedition circumnavigates it; he proves the doctrine of the antipodes, for he sees the men of the antipodes;[2] but even this does not end the war. Many earnest and good men oppose the doctrine for two hundred years longer. Then the French astronomers make their measurements of degrees in equatorial and polar regions, and add to other proofs that of the lengthened pendulum : when

---

[1] See *Daunou, Études Historiques*, vol. ii., p. 417.

[2] For effect of Magalhaens's voyages, and the reluctance to yield to proof, see *Henri Martin, Histoire de France*, vol. xiv., p. 395; *St. Martin's Histoire de la Géog.*, p. 369; *Peschel, Geschichte des Zeitalters der Entdeckungen*, concluding chapters; and for an admirable summary, *Draper, Hist. Int. Dev. of Europe*, pp. 451-453.

this was done, when the deductions of science were seen to be established by the simple test of measurement, beautifully, perfectly, then and then only this war of twelve centuries ended.[1]

And now, what was the result of this war? The efforts of Eusebius and Lactantius to deaden scientific thought; the efforts of Augustine to combat it; the efforts of Cosmas to stop it by dogmatism; the efforts of Boniface, and Zachary, and others to stop it by force, conscientious as they all were, had resulted in what? Simply in forcing into many noble minds this most unfortunate conviction, that Science and Religion are enemies; simply in driving away from religion hosts of the best men in all those centuries. The result was wholly bad. No optimism can change that verdict.

On the other hand, what was gained by the warriors of science for religion? Simply, a far more ennobling conception of the world, and a far truer conception of Him who made and who sustains it.

Which is the more consistent with a great, true religion—the cosmography of Cosmas, or that of Isaac Newton? Which presents the nobler food

---

[1] For general statement as to supplementary proof by measurement of degrees, and by pendulum, see *Somerville, Phys. Geog.*, chapter i., § 6, note. Also *Humboldt, Cosmos*, vol. ii., p. 736, and v., pp. 16, 32. Also *Montucla*, iv., 138.

for religious thought—the diatribes of Lactantius, or the astronomical discourses of Thomas Chalmers?

ASTRONOMY.

The next great battle was fought on a question relating to the *position of the earth among the heavenly bodies*. On one side, the great body of conscientious religious men planted themselves firmly on the geocentric doctrine—the doctrine that the earth is the centre, and that the sun and planets revolve about it. The doctrine was old, and of the highest respectability.[1] The very name, Ptolemaic theory, carried weight. It had been elaborated until it accounted well for the phenomena. Exact textual interpreters of Scripture cherished it, for it agreed with the letter of the sacred text.[2]

But, most important of all, it was stamped with the seal of St. Thomas Aquinas. The sainted theologian—the glory of the Mediæval Church, the "angelic doctor"—he to whom it was believed an

---

[1] *Respectability of Geocentric Theory, Plato's Authority for it* etc., see *Grote's Plato*, vol. iii., p. 257. Also, *Sir G. C. Lewis, Astronomy of the Ancients*, chap. iii., sec. i., for a very thoughtful statement of Plato's view, and differing from ancient statements. For plausible elaboration of it, see *Fromundus, Anti-Aristarchus*, Antwerp, 1631. Also *Melanchthon, Initia Doctrinæ Physicæ*.

[2] For supposed agreement of Scripture with Ptolemaic theory, see Fromundus, *passim*, Melanchthon, and a host of other writers.

image of the Crucified had spoken words praising his writings—had shown in his treatise on the Heaven and Earth, by philosophy, theology, and revelation, that the position of the earth must be in the centre.[1]

Still the germs of the heliocentric theory[2] had been planted long before, and well planted; it had seemed ready even to bloom forth in the fifth century, from the mind of Martianus Capella, and in the fifteenth from the mind of Cardinal de Cusa; but it could not be forgotten that St. Thomas had elaborated the opposite view; the chill of dogmatism was still over the earth, and up to the beginning of the sixteenth century there had come to this great truth neither bloom nor fruitage.[3]

[1] See *St. Thomas Aquinas, Liber de Cœlo et Mundo*, sec. xx.
[2] For *Germs of Heliocentric Theory planted long before*, etc., see Sir G. C. Lewis; also, Draper, *Intellectual Developement of Europe*, p. 512; and for a succinct statement of the claims of Pythagoras, Philolaus, Aristarchus, and Martianus Capella, see *Hœfer, Hist. de l'Astronomie*, 1873, p. 107, *et seq.* For germs among thinkers of India, see *Whewell*, vol. i., p. 277. Also, Whitney, *Oriental and Linguistic Studies*, New York, 1874; *Essay on the Lunar Zodiac*, p. 345.
[3] For general statement of De Cusa's work, see *Draper, Intellectual Development of Europe*, p. 512. For skillful use of De Cusa's view in order to mitigate censure upon the Church for its treatment of Copernicus's discovery, see an article in the *Catholic World* for January, 1869. For a very exact statement, in a spirit of judicial fairness, see *Whewell, History of the Inductive Sciences*, p. 275 and pp. 379, 380. In the latter, Whewell cites the exact

Quietly, however, the soil was receiving enrichment, and the air warmth. The processes of mathematics were constantly improved, the heavenly bodies were steadily though silently observed; and at length appeared, afar off from the centres of thought, on the borders of Poland, a plain, simple-minded scholar, who first fairly uttered to the world the truth, now so commonplace, then so astounding, that the sun and planets do not revolve about the earth, but that the earth and planets revolve about the sun, and that man was Nicholas Kopernik.[1]

Kopernik had been a professor at Rome, but,

---

words of De Cusa in the *De Docta Ignorantia*, and sums up in these words: "This train of thought might be a preparation for the reception of the Copernican system; but it is very different from the doctrine that the sun is the centre of the planetary system." In the previous passage, Whewell says that De Cusa "propounded the doctrine of the motion of the earth, more, however, as a paradox than as a reality. We cannot consider this as any distinct anticipation of a profound and consistent view of the truth." For Aristotle's views and their elaboration by St. Thomas Aquinas, see the treatise *De Cœlo et Mundo*. It is curious to see how even such a biographer of St. Thomas as Archbishop Vaughan slurs over the angelic docter's errors. See *Vaughan's Life and Labors of St. Thomas of Aquin*, pp. 459, 460.

[1] For improvement of mathematical processes, see *Draper, Intellectual Development of Europe*, 513. In looking at this and other admirable summaries, one feels that Prof. Tyndall was not altogether right in lamenting, in his farewell address at New York, that Dr. Draper has devoted so much of his time to historical studies.

as this truth grew within him, he seemed to feel that at Rome he was no longer safe.[1]

To publish this thought was dangerous indeed, and for more than thirty years it lay slumbering in the minds of Kopernik and the friends to whom he had privately intrusted it.

[1] Kopernik's danger at Rome. The *Catholic World* for January, 1869, cites a recent speech of the Archbishop of Mechlin before the University of Louvain, to the effect that Copernicus defended his theory, at Rome, in 1500, before two thousand scholars; also, that another professor taught the system in 1528, and was made Apostolic Notary by Clement VIII. All this, even if the doctrines taught were identical with those of Copernicus, as finally developed, which idea Whewell seems utterly to disprove, avails nothing against the overwhelming testimony that Copernicus felt himself in danger—testimony which the after-history of the Copernican theory renders invincible. The very title of Fromundus's book, already cited, published within a few miles of the archbishop's own cathedral, and sanctioned expressly by the theological Faculty of that same University of Louvain in 1630, utterly refutes the archbishop's idea that the Church was inclined to treat Copernicus kindly. The title is as follows:

"Anti-Aristarchus | Sive | Orbis-Terræ | Immobilis | In quo decretum S. Congregationis S. R. E. | Cardinalium | IꝰC. XVI adversus Pytha | gorico-Copernicanos editum defenditur | Antwerpiæ MDCXXXI."

L'Epinois, Galilée, Paris, 1867, lays stress, p. 14, on the broaching of the doctrine by De Cusa, in 1435, and by Widmanstadt, in 1533, and their kind treatment by Eugenius IV. and Clement VII. But this is absolutely worthless in denying the papal policy afterward. *Lange, Geschichte des Materialismus*, vol. i., pp. 217, 218, while admitting that De Cusa and Widmanstadt sustained this idea and received honors from their respective popes, shows that,

At last he prepares his great work on the *Revolution of the Heavenly Bodies*, and dedicates it to the pope himself. He next seeks a place of publication. He dares not send it to Rome, for there are the rulers of the older Church ready to seize it. He dares not send it to Wittenberg, for there are the leaders of Protestantism no less hostile. It is therefore intrusted to Osiander, of Nuremberg.[1]

But, at the last moment, Osiander's courage fails him. He dares not launch the new thought boldly. He writes a groveling preface; endeavors to excuse Kopernik for his novel idea. He inserts the apologetic lie that Kopernik propounds the doctrine of the movement of the earth, not as a *fact*, but as an *hypothesis;* he declares that it is lawful for an astronomer to indulge his *imagination*, and that this is what Kopernik has done.

Thus was the greatest and most ennobling, perhaps, of scientific truths—a truth not less enno-

when the Church gave it serious consideration, it was condemned. There is nothing in this view unreasonable. It would be a parallel case to that of Leo X., at first inclined toward Luther and the others, in their "squabbles with the begging friars," and afterward forced to oppose them. That Copernicus felt the danger, is evident, among other things, by the expression in the preface, "*Statim me explodendum cum tali opinione clamitant.*"

[1] For dangers at Wittenberg, see *Lange, Geschichte des Materialismus*, vol. i., p. 217.

bling to religion than to science—forced, in coming into the world, to sneak and crawl.[1]

On the 24th of May, 1543, the newly-printed book first arrived at the house of Kopernik. It was put into his hands; but he was on his deathbed. A few hours later he was beyond the reach of those mistaken, conscientious men, whose consciences would have blotted his reputation, and perhaps have destroyed his life.

Yet not wholly beyond their reach. Even death could not be trusted to shield him. There seems to have been fear of vengeance upon his corpse, for on his tombstone was placed no record of his life-long labors, no mention of his great

---

[1] Osiander, in a letter to Copernicus, dated April 20, 1541, had endeavored to reconcile him to such a procedure, and ends by saying, "Sic enim placidiores reddideris peripatheticos et theologos quos contradicturos metuis." See *Apologia Tychonis* in *Kepleri Opera Omnia*, Frisch's edition, vol. i., p. 246. Kepler holds Osiander entirely responsible for this preface. Bertrand, in his *Fondateurs de l'Astronomie Moderne*, gives its text, and thinks it possible that Copernicus may have yielded "in pure condescension toward his disciple." But this idea is utterly at variance with expressions in Copernicus's own dedicatory letter to the pope, which follows the preface. For a good summary of the argument, see *Figuier, Savants de la Renaissance*, pp. 378, 379. See, also, citation from Gassendi's life of Copernicus, in *Flammarion, Vie de Copernic*, p. 124. Mr. John Fiske, accurate as he usually is, in his recent *Outlines of Cosmic Philosophy*, appears to have followed Laplace, Delambre, and Petit into the error of supposing that Copernicus, and not Osiander, is responsible for the preface.

discovery. There were graven upon it affecting words, which may be thus simply translated: "I ask not the grace accorded to Paul, not that given to Peter; give me only the favor which thou didst show to the thief on the cross." Not till thirty years after did a friend dare write on his tombstone a memorial of his discovery.[1]

The book was taken in hand by the proper authorities. In due time it was solemnly condemned; to read it was to risk damnation; and the world accepted the decree.[2] The earnest theo-

---

[1] *Figuier, Savants de la Renaissance*, p. 380. Also, *Flammarion, Vie de Copernic*, p. 190.

[2] The "proper authorities" in this case were the "Congregation of the Index," or cardinals having charge of the "Index Librorum Prohibitorum." Recent desperate attempts to fasten the responsibility on them as individuals seem ridiculous in view of the simple fact that their work is sanctioned by the highest Church authority, and required to be universally accepted by the Church. Three of four editions of the "Index" in my own possession declare on their title-pages that they are issued by order of the pontiff of the period, and each is prefaced by a special papal bull or letter. See, especially, Index of 1664, issued under order of Alexander VII., and that of 1761, under Benedict XIV. Copernicus's work was prohibited in the Index "*donec corrigatur*." Kepler said that it ought to be worded "*donec explicetur*." See *Bertrand, Fondateurs de l'Astronomie Moderne*, p. 57. *De Morgan*, pp. 57–60, gives the corrections required by the Index of 1620. Their main aim seems to be to reduce Copernicus to the groveling level of Osiander, making of his discovery a mere hypothesis; but occasionally they require a virtual giving up of the whole Copernican doctrine, e. g., "correction" insisted upon for

logians of the period immediately wheeled their batteries of sacred learning to support the Church in its effort to beat back the terrible doctrine that the earth revolves about the sun. Among the most vigorous of them in Northern Europe was Fromundus. From the shadow of the Cathedral of Antwerp he sent forth his famous treatise, the *Anti-Aristarchus*, full of the strongest arguments against the new theory. His very title-page was a contemptuous insult to the memory of Kopernik, since it paraded the assumption that the new truth was only an old and exploded theory of Aristarchus. He declares that "sacred Scripture fights against the Copernicans." To prove that the sun revolves about the earth, he cites the passage in the Psalms which speaks of the sun "which cometh forth as a bridegroom out of his chamber." To prove that the earth stands still, he quotes the passage from Ecclesiastes, "the earth standeth fast forever." To show the utter futility of the Copernican ideas, he indulges in scientific reasoning as he understands it—declaring that, if the hated theory were true, "the wind would constantly blow from the east; we should with great difficulty hear sounds against such a wind;" that "buildings, and the earth itself,

cap. 8, p. 6. For scholarly account of the relation of the Prohibitory and Expurgatory Indexes to each other, see Mendham, *Literary Policy of the Church of Rome.*

would fly off with such a rapid motion;" and, greatest weapon of all, he works up, by the use of Aristotle and Thomas Aquinas, a demonstration from theology and science combined, that the earth must stand in the centre, and that the sun must revolve about it.[1]

Doubtless many will at once exclaim against the Roman Catholic Church for this. Justice compels me to say that the founders of Protestantism were no less zealous against the new scientific doctrine. Said Martin Luther: "People gave ear to an upstart astrologer, who strove to show that the earth revolves, not the heavens or the firmament, the sun and the moon. Whoever wishes to appear clever must devise some new system, which of all systems is, of course, the very best. This fool wishes to reverse the entire science of astronomy. But Sacred Scripture tells us that Joshua commanded the sun to stand still, and not the earth."

Melanchthon, mild as he was, was not behind Luther in condemning Kopernik. In his treatise, *Initia Doctrinæ Physicæ*, he says: "The eyes are

---

[1] See Fromundus's book, cited above, *passim*, but especially the heading of chapter vi., and the argument in chaps. x. and xi. For interesting reference to one of Fromundus's arguments, showing by a mixture of mathematics and theology, that the earth is the centre of the universe, see Quetelet, *Histoire des Sciences Mathématiques et Physiques*, Bruxelles, 1864, p. 170.

witnesses that the heavens revolve in the space of twenty-four hours. But certain men, either from the love of novelty, or to make a display of ingenuity, have concluded that the earth moves; and they maintain that neither the eighth sphere nor the sun revolves. . . . Now, it is a want of honesty and decency to assert such notions publicly, and the example is pernicious. It is the part of a good mind to accept the truth as revealed by God, and to acquiesce in it." Melanchthon then cites passages from the Psalms and from Ecclesiastes - which he declares assert positively and clearly that the earth stands fast, and that the sun moves around it, and adds eight other proofs of his proposition that "the earth can be nowhere, if not in the centre of the universe."[1]

And Protestant people were not a whit behind Catholic in following out these teachings. The people of Elbing made themselves merry over a farce in which Kopernik was the main object of ridicule. The people of Nuremberg, a great Prot-

[1] See *Luther's Tischreden, Irmischer's Ausgabe*. Also, *Melanchthon's Initia Doctrinæ Physicæ*. This treatise is cited under a mistaken title by the *Catholic World*, September, 1870. The correct title is as given above. It will be found in the *Corpus Reformatorum*, ed. *Bretschneider*, Halle, 1846. (For the above passage, see vol. xiii., pp. 216, 217.) Also, *Lange, Geschichte des Materialismus*, vol. i., p. 217. Also, *Prowe, Ueber die Abhängigkeit des Copernicus*, Thorn, 1865, p. 4. Also, note, pp. 5 and 6, where text is given in full.

estant centre, caused a medal to be struck, with inscriptions ridiculing the philosopher and his theory.[1]

Then was tried, also, one piece of strategy very common formerly in battles between theologians themselves. It consists in loud shoutings that the doctrine attacked is outworn, and already refuted—that various distinguished gentlemen have proved it false—that it is not a living truth, but a detected lie—that, if the world listens to it, that is simply because the world is ignorant. This strategy was brought to bear on Kopernik. It was shown that his doctrine was simply a revival of the Pythagorean notion, which had been thoroughly exploded. Fromundus, as we have seen in his title-page and throughout his book, delights in referring to the doctrine of .the revolution of the planets around the sun, as " that Pythagorean notion." This mode of warfare was imitated by the lesser opponents, and produced, for some time, considerable effect.[2]

But the new truth could neither be laughed down nor forced down. Many minds had received it; only one tongue dared utter it. This new warrior was that strange mortal, Giordano Bruno.

[1] For treatment of Copernican ideas by the people, see *Catholic World*, as above.

[2] See title-page of Fromundus's work cited in note at bottom of p. 392; also, Melanchthon, *ubi supra*.

He was hunted from land to land, until, at last, he turns on his pursuers with fearful invectives. For this he is imprisoned six years, then burned alive and his ashes scattered to the winds. Still the new truth lived on; it could not be killed. Within ten years after the martyrdom of Bruno,[1] after a world of troubles and persecutions, the truth of the doctrine of Kopernik was established by the telescope of Galileo.[2]

Herein was fulfilled one of the most touching of prophecies. Years before, the enemies of Kopernik had said to him, "If your doctrines were true, Venus would show phases like the moon." Kopernik answered: "You are right; I know not what to say; but God is good, and will in time find an answer to this objection."[3] The God-

---

[1] See *Bartholmess, Vie de Jordano Bruno*, Paris, 1846, vol. i., pp. 121 and pp. 212, *et seq.* Also *Berti, Vita di Giordano Bruno*, Firenze, 1868, chapter xvi. Also *Whewell*, i., 294, 295. That Whewell is somewhat hasty in attributing Bruno's punishment entirely to the *Spaccio della Bestia Trionfante* will be evident, in spite of Montucla, to any one who reads the account of the persecution in Bartholmess or Berti; and, even if Whewell be right, the *Spaccio* would never have been written, but for Bruno's indignation at ecclesiastical oppression. See *Tiraboschi*, vol. xi., p. 435.

[2] *Delambre, Histoire de l'Astronomie moderne*, discours préliminaire, p. xiv. Also *Laplace, Système du Monde*, vol. i., p. 326, and for more careful statement, *Kepleri Opera Omnia*, edit. Frisch, tom. ii., p. 464.

[3] *Cantu, Histoire Universelle*, vol. xv., p. 473.

given answer came when the rude telescope of Galileo showed the phases of Venus.

On this new champion, Galileo, the war was long and bitter. The supporters of what was called "sound learning" declared his discoveries deceptions, and his announcements blasphemy. Semi-scientific professors, endeavoring to curry favor with the Church, attacked him with sham science; earnest preachers attacked him with perverted Scripture![1]

I shall present this warfare at some length, because, so far as I can find, no careful outline of it has been given in our language, since the whole history was placed in a new light by the revelation of the trial documents in the Vatican Library, published for the first time by M. de l'Epinois in 1867.

The first important attack on Galileo began when he announced that his telescope had revealed

---

[1] A very curious example of this sham science is seen in the argument, frequently used at the time, that, if the earth really moved, a stone falling from a height would fall back of the point immediately below its point of starting. This is used by Fromundus with great effect. It appears never to have occurred to him to test the matter by dropping a stone from the topmast of a ship. But the most beautiful thing of all is that Benzenburg has experimentally demonstrated just such an aberration in falling bodies as is mathematically required by the diurnal motion of the earth. See *Jevons, Principles of Science*, vol. i., p. 453, and ii., pp. 310, 311.

the moons of the planet Jupiter; the enemy saw that this strengthened the Copernican theory, and gave battle immediately.

The whole theory was denounced as impossible and impious. Professors, bred in the mixed science favored by the Church,[1] argued that the Bible clearly showed, by all applicable types, that there could be only seven planets; that this was proved by the seven golden candlesticks of the Apocalypse, by the seven-branched candlestick of the Tabernacle, and by the seven churches of Asia:[2] theologians showed the destructive consequences which must logically result to fundamental Christian truths: bishops and priests uttered impressive warnings to their flocks; and multitudes of the faithful besought the Inquisition to protect the fold by dealing speedily and sharply with the heretic.

In vain did Galileo try to save the great truths he had discovered, by his letters to the Benedictine Castelli and the Grand-duchess Christine, in which he argued that literal Biblical interpretation should not be applied to science; it was declared that by making such an argument his heresy was only

---

[1] See Delambre as to the discovery of the satellites of Jupiter being the turning-point with the heliocentric doctrine. As to its effects on Bacon, see *Jevons, Principles of Science*, vol. ii., p. 298.

[2] For argument drawn from the candlestick and seven churches, see Delambre.

rendered more detestable; that he was "worse than Luther or Calvin."

In vain did he try to prove the existence of satellites by showing them to the doubters through his telescope. They either declared it impious to look, or, if they did see them, denounced them as illusions from the devil. Good Father Clavius declared that to "see satellites of Jupiter, men had to make an instrument which would create them." [1]

The war on the Copernican theory, which up to that time had been carried on quietly, now flamed forth. It was declared that the doctrine was proved false by the standing still of the sun for Joshua; by the declarations that "the foundations of the earth are fixed so firm that they cannot be moved," and that the sun "runneth about from one end of heaven to the other." [2]

The Dominican father, Caccini, preached a sermon from the text, "Ye men of Galilee, why stand ye gazing up into heaven?" and this wretched pun was the first of a series of sharper weapons; for before Caccini finishes, he insists that "geometry is of the devil," and that "mathematicians

---

[1] *Libri*, vol. iv., p. 211. *De Morgan, Paradoxes*, p. 26, for account of Father Clavius. It is interesting to know that Clavius, in his last years, acknowledged that "the whole system of the heavens is broken down, and must be mended."

[2] *Cantu, Histoire Universelle*, vol. xv., p. 478.

should be banished as the authors of all heresies;" and, for this, the Church authorities gave Caccini promotion.'

Father Lorini proved that the doctrine was not only "heretical," but "atheistic," and besought the Inquisition to intervene. The Bishop of Fiesole screamed in rage against the Copernican system, and proposed to denounce Galileo to the grandduke. The Archbishop of Pisa secretly sought to entrap Galileo and deliver him to the Inquisition at Rome. The Archbishop of Florence solemnly condemned the doctrines of Kopernik and Galileo as unscriptural.

But by far the most terrible champion who appeared against him was Bellarmin, one of the greatest of theologians, and one of the poorest of scientists. He was earnest, sincere, learned, but made the fearful mistake for the world of applying to science, direct, literal interpretation of Scripture.[2]

The weapons which men of Bellarmin's stamp used were theological. They held up before the world the dreadful consequences which must result

---

[1] For Caccini's attack, see *Delambre, Hist. de l'Astron.*, disc. prélim., p. xxii.; also, *Libri, Hist. des Sciences Math.*, vol. iv., p. 232; also, *Martin, Galilée*, pp. 43, 44.

[2] For Bellarmin's view, see *Quinet, Jesuits*, vol. ii., p. 189. For other objectors and objections, see *Libri, Histoire des Sciences Mathématiques en Italie*, vol. iv., pp. 233, 234; also, *Martin, Vie de Galilée*.

to Christian theology were the doctrine to prevail that the heavenly bodies revolve about the sun, and not about the earth. Their most tremendous theologic engine against Galileo was the idea that his pretended discovery "vitiated the whole Christian plan of salvation." Father Lecazre declared that it "cast suspicion on the doctrine of the Incarnation." Others declared that it "upset the whole basis of theology; that, if the earth is a planet, and one among several planets, it cannot be that any such great things have been done especially for it, as the Christian doctrine teaches. If there are other planets, since God makes nothing in vain, they must be inhabited; but how can these inhabitants be descended from Adam? How can they trace back their origin to Noah's ark? How can they have been redeemed by the Saviour?"[1]

Nor was this argument confined to the theologians of the Roman Church; Melanchthon, Protestant as he was, had already used it in his attacks upon the ideas of Kopernik and his school.[2]

In addition to this prodigious engine of war, there was kept up a terrific fire of smaller artillery in the shape of texts and scriptural extracts.

But the little telescope of Galileo still swept

[1] See Trouessart, cited in *Flammarion, Mondes Imaginaires et Réels*, sixième édition, pp. 315, 316.
[2] *Initia Doctrinæ Physicæ*, pp. 220, 221.

the heavens, and the next revelation announced was the system of mountains and valleys in the moon. This was a signal for another attack. It was declared that this, coupled with the statement that the moon shines by light reflected from the sun, was a contradiction of the statement in Genesis that the moon is a "great light" like the sun. To make the matter worse, a painter, placing the moon in a religious picture in its usual position beneath the feet of the Blessed Virgin, outlined on its surface mountains and valleys; this was denounced as a sacrilege logically resulting from the astronomer's heresy.

The next struggle was aroused when the hated telescope revealed spots upon the sun, and their motion, which indicated the sun's rotation. Monsignor Elci, head of the University of Pisa, forbade the Professor of Astronomy, Castelli, to mention these spots. Father Busaeus, at the University of Innspruck, forbade the astronomer Scheiner to allow the new discovery to be known there. At the College of Douay and the University of Louvain it was expressly placed under the ban, and this became the general rule among the Catholic universities and colleges of Europe. The Spanish universities were specially intolerant of this and similar ideas,¹ and up to a recent period they were

---

† See Ticknor, *Hist. of Span. Literature*, vol. iii.

strictly forbidden in the most important university of all—that of Salamanca. In 1820 the Abbé Settele, professor at the College of Rome, having announced a work on Optics and Astronomy, the master of the sacred palace, under the authority of the old decrees against the teachings of Kopernik and Galileo, forbade the publication, and it was not until 1822 that Pope Pius VII. sanctioned a decision of the Inquisition permitting such teachings.[1]

Such are the consequences of placing the instruction of men's minds in the hands of those mainly absorbed in the work of saving men's souls.[2] Nothing could be more in accordance with the idea recently put forth by the Bishop of Montpellier, that the Church is alone fully empowered to promulgate scientific truth or direct university instruction; but science gained the victory here also. News came of observations of the solar spots, not only from Galileo in Italy, but from Fabricius in Holland. Father Scheiner then endeavors to make the usual treaty; he promulgates a pseudo-scientific theory—a statement based on a "religious science"—which only provokes derision.

But the war grew more and more bitter, and

[1] See *Th. Martin, Galilée*, pp 34, 208, and 266.
[2] See *Martin, Galilée*, pp. 34 and 208; also a curious note in the earlier English editions, *Lyell, Principles of Geology*, Introduction.

the principal weapons in it are worth examining. They are very easily examined; you may pick them up on any of the battle-fields of science; but on that field they were used with more effect than on almost any other. These weapons are two epithets: "Infidel" and "Atheist."

The battle-fields of science are thickly strewn with these. They have been used against almost every man who has ever done anything new for his fellow-men. The list of those who have been denounced as infidel and atheist includes almost all great men of science—general scholars, inventors, philanthropists. The deepest Christian life, the most noble Christian character, have not availed to shield combatants. Christians like Isaac Newton and Pascal and John Locke and John Milton, and even Howard and Fénelon, have had these weapons hurled against them. Of all proofs of the existence of a God, those of Descartes have been wrought most thoroughly into the minds of modern men; and yet the Protestant theologians of Holland sought to bring him to torture and to death by the charge of atheism, and the Roman Catholic theologians of France prevented the rendering of any due honors to him at his burial.[1]

[1] For curious exemplification of the way in which these weapons have been hurled, see lists of persons charged with "infidelity" and "atheism," in *Le Dictionnaire des Athées*, Paris, An. viii. Also, Lecky, *History of Rationalism*, vol. ii., p. 50. For case of Descartes, see *Saisset, Descartes et ses precurseurs*, pp. 103, 110.

These epithets can hardly be classed with civilized weapons. They are burning arrows. They set fire to great masses of popular prejudices; smoke rises to obscure the real questions; fire bursts forth at times to destroy the attacked party. They are poisoned. They go to the hearts of loving women, they alienate dear children; they injure the man after life is ended, for they leave poisoned wounds in the hearts of those who loved him best—fears for his eternal happiness—dread of the Divine displeasure. Of course, in these days, these weapons, though often effective in disturbing good men and in scaring good women, are somewhat blunted. Indeed, they not unfrequently injure assailants more than assailed. So it was not in the days of Galileo; they were then in all their sharpness and venom.

Yet far more vile than the use even of these weapons—vile indeed beyond belief—was the attack by the Archbishop of Pisa.

It is a remark made by one of the most moderate and judicially fair of modern philosophic historians, that, of all organizations this world has known, the Roman Church has caused most undeserved woe and shed most innocent blood; but, in the whole terrible succession of Torquemadas and Arbues and Granvilles, the vilest enemy of the human race is probably this same Archbishop of Pisa.

This man, whose cathedral is more truly consecrated by the remembrance of Galileo's observation of the lamp swinging before its altar, than by all the church services of a thousand years, began a siege against the great philosopher.

Galileo, after his discoveries had been denounced as contrary to Scripture, had been induced to write to the Duchess Christine and to his friend Castelli two letters, to show that his discoveries might be reconciled to Scripture. The archbishop saw his opportunity: he determined to get hold of these letters and exhibit them as proofs that Galileo had uttered heretical views of theology and the Scriptures, and thus to bring the astronomer hopelessly into the clutch of the Inquisition. The archbishop begs Castelli, therefore, to let him see the original letter in the handwriting of Galileo. Castelli declines; the archbishop then, while, as is now revealed, writing constantly and bitterly to the inquisitors against Galileo, professes to Castelli the greatest admiration of Galileo's genius, and a sincere desire to know more of his discoveries. Castelli is seduced by this; but Galileo sturdily forbids sending the letter, and the archbishop is obliged to resort to open attack.

The whole struggle to crush Galileo and to save him would be amusing were it not so fraught with evil. There were intrigues and counter-intrigues, plots and counter-plots, lying and spying.

and in the thickest of this seething, squabbling, screaming mass, priests, bishops, archbishops, cardinals, and even the future Pope Urban VIII. himself. It is most suggestive to see in this crisis of the Church, on the eve of the greatest errors in church policy the world has known, in all the efforts and deliberations of these consecrated leaders of the Church, at the tomb of the Prince of the Apostles, no more sign of the guidance or presence of the Holy Spirit than in a caucus of New York politicians.

But the opposing powers were too strong. In 1615 Galileo is summoned by the Inquisition to Rome, and the mine, which had been so long preparing, was sprung. Pope Paul V. and the cardinal inquisitors order eleven theologians of the Inquisition to examine these two propositions which had been extracted from Galileo's letters on the solar spots: *First*, that the sun does not move about the earth; *secondly*, that the earth does move about the sun. The eleven theologians solemnly considered these points, and in about a month rendered a solemn decision that "the first proposition, *that the sun is the centre, and does not revolve about the earth, is foolish, absurd, false in theology, and heretical, because expressly contrary to Holy Scripture; and that the second proposition, that the earth is not the centre, but revolves about the sun, is absurd, false in philosophy, and, from a theological point of view, at least opposed to the true faith."* [1]

The pope himself, Paul V., now intervenes; he orders that Galileo be brought before the Inquisition. Then the great man of science in that age is brought face to face with the greatest theologian: Galileo is confronted by Cardinal Bellarmin. Bellarmin shows Galileo the error of his opinion, and orders him to renounce it. De Lauda, fortified by a letter from the pope, ordering the astronomer to be placed in the dungeon of the Inquisition should he refuse to yield, commands him to "*abandon entirely the opinion that the sun is the centre of the universe, and that the earth moves,* and to abstain from sustaining, teaching, or defending that opinion in any manner whatever, orally or by writing." [2]

Galileo bowed to this order, was allowed to retire, and the whole proceeding was kept secret.

About ten days later, on March 5, 1616, the Congregation of the Index, moved thereto, as we have seen, and as the letters and documents now brought to light show, by Pope Paul V., solemnly rendered their decree: that the doctrine of the double movement of the earth about its axis and about the sun is *false and entirely contrary*

---

[1] See the original documents in *Epinois*, pp. 34-36. Martin's translation does not seem exactly correct.

[2] See full official text in *Epinois*.

to Holy Scripture; that this opinion must neither be taught nor defended. The same decree condemned the writings of Kopernik, and *all writings which affirm the motion of the earth.* The great work of Kopernik was interdicted until corrected in accordance with the views of the Inquisition; and the works of Galileo and Kepler, though not mentioned by name, were included among those implicitly condemned as "affirming the motion of the earth."

The condemnations were inscribed upon the *Index*, and to the Index was prefixed the usual papal bull giving its monitions the papal sanction. To teach or even read the works denounced or passages condemned, was to risk persecution in this world and damnation in the next. Human science had apparently lost the great decisive battle.

For some time Galileo remained at Rome perfectly submissive.[1] Pope Paul V. petted him, and all seemed happy in the ending of the long war.

But, returning to Florence, something of his old scientific ardor stirred within him; and at last Cardinal Barberini, who had seemed liberal and friendly, having been made pope under the name

[1] See proofs of this in *Martin*. The reader should be reminded that the archives exposed within the past few years have made the statements of early writers untrustworthy on very many of the nicer points.

of Urban VIII., Galileo conceived new hopes, and again in a published work alluded favorably to the Copernican system. New troubles ensued. Galileo was induced to visit Rome again, and Pope Urban tried to cajole him into silence, and personally took the trouble to try to show the astronomer his errors by argument. Other opponents were less considerate. Works appeared attacking his ideas—works all the more unmanly, since their authors knew how Galileo was restrained by force from defending himself; and, as if to accumulate proofs of the fitness of the Church to take charge of advanced instruction, his salary as professor at the University of Pisa was taken from him. Sapping and mining began. Just as the Archbishop of Pisa some years before had tried to betray Galileo with honeyed words to the Inquisition, so now Father Grassi tried it; and after various attempts to draw him out by flattery, suddenly denounced his scientific ideas as "leading to a denial of the real presence in the Eucharist."

And here science again loses' ground. Galileo had announced his intention of writing upon the theory of the tides, but he retreated, and thus was lost a great treatise to the world.

For the final assault, the park of heavy artillery was at last wheeled into place. You see it on all the scientific battle-fields. It consists of general denunciation; and Father Melchior Inchofer, of the Jesuits, brought his artillery to bear well on Galileo with this declaration: that the opinion of the earth's motion is, of all heresies, the most abominable, the most pernicious, the most scandalous; that the immobility of the earth is thrice sacred; that argument against the immortality of the soul, the Creator, the incarnation, etc., should be tolerated sooner than an argument to prove that the earth moves.'

But this state of things could not be endured forever. Urged beyond forbearance, Galileo prepares a careful treatise in the form of a dialogue, exhibiting the arguments for and against the Copernican and Ptolemaic systems. He then offers to submit to any conditions the Church tribunals may impose, if they will but allow it to be printed. At last they consent, imposing the most humiliating condition of all, which was a preface written by Father Ricciardi and signed by Galileo, in which the whole work was virtually exhibited as a play of the imagination, and not at all as opposed to the truth laid down in 1616 by the Inquisition.

The new work met with prodigious success; it put new weapons into the hands of the supporters of the Copernican theory. The preface only embittered the contest; it was laughed at from one

[1] See *Inchofer's Tractatus Syllepticus*, cited in Galileo's letter to Deodati, July 28, 1634.

end of Europe to the other as ironical. This aroused the enemy. The Jesuits, Dominicans, and the great majority of the clergy, returned to the attack more violent than ever; and Pope Urban VIII., his personal pride being touched, after some halting joined the clerical forces.

The first important piece of strategy was to forbid the sale of the work; but the first edition had already been exhausted and spread throughout Europe. Urban now became angry, and both Galileo and his works were placed in the hands of the Inquisition. In vain did the good Benedictine Castelli urge that Galileo was entirely respectful to the Church; in vain did he say that "nothing that could be done could now hinder the earth from revolving." He was dismissed, and Galileo was forced to appear in the presence of the dread tribunal without defender or adviser. There, as was so long concealed but as is now fully revealed, he was menaced with torture by express order of Pope Urban, and, as is now thoroughly established by documentary evidence, forced to abjure under threats, and subjected to imprisonment by command of Urban, the Inquisition deferring in the most servile manner to the papal authority.

The rest of the story the world knows by heart; none of the recent attempts have succeeded in mystifying it. The whole world will remember forever how Galileo was subjected certainly to indignity and imprisonment equivalent to physical torture;[1] how he was at last forced to pronounce publicly, and on his knees, his recantation as follows: "I, Galileo, being in my seventieth year, being a prisoner and on my knees, and before your eminences, having before my eyes the Holy Gospel, which I touch with my hands, abjure, curse, and detest the error and the heresy of the movement of the earth."

He was vanquished indeed, for he had been forced, in the face of all coming ages, to perjure himself; and, to complete his dishonor, he was obliged to swear to denounce to the Inquisition any other man of science whom he should discover to be supporting heresy—the "heresy of the movement of the earth."

Nor was this all. To the end of his life, nay, after his life was ended, this bitter persecution was continued, on the supposition that the great truths he revealed were hurtful to religion. After a brief stay in the dungeons of the Inquisition, he was kept in exile from family, friends, all his noble employments, and held rigidly to his promise not even to speak of his theory. When,

---

[1] It is not probable that torture in the ordinary sense was administered to Galileo, though it was threatened. See *Th. Martin, Vie de Galilée*, for a fair summing up of the case. For text of the abjuration, see *Epinois*; also, *Private Life of Galileo*, Appendix.

in the midst of intense bodily sufferings from disease and mental sufferings from calamities in his family, he besought some little liberty, he was met with threats of a recommittal to his dungeon. When, at last, a special commissioner had reported to the ecclesiastical authorities that Galileo had become blind and wasted away with disease and sorrow, he was allowed but little more liberty, and that little tempered by the close surveillance of the ecclesiastical authorities. He was forced to bear contemptible attacks on himself and on his works in silence; he lived to see his ideas carefully weeded out from all the church colleges and universities in Europe; and when, in a scientific work, he happened to be spoken of as " renowned," the Inquisition ordered the substitution of the word "notorious." [1]

Nor did the persecution cease with his death. Galileo had begged to be buried in his family tomb in Santa Croce; the request was denied: his friends wished to erect a monument over him; this, too, was refused. Pope Urban said to the embassador Niccolini that "it would be an evil example for the world if such honors were rendered to a man who had been brought before the Roman Inquisition for an opinion so false and erroneous, who had communicated it to many

[1] *Martin*, p. 227.

others, and who had given so great a scandal to Christendom." [1]

In accordance, therefore, with the wish of the pope and the orders of the Inquisition, Galileo was buried ignobly, apart from his family, without fitting ceremony, without monument, without epitaph. Not until forty years after did Pierozzi dare to write his epitaph. Not until a hundred years after did Nelli dare transfer his remains to Santa Croce and erect above them a suitable monument. Even then the old conscientious hostility burst out: the Inquisition was besought to prevent such honors to "a man condemned for notorious errors;" and that tribunal refused to allow any epitaph to be placed above him which had not first been submitted to its censorship. Nor has that old conscientious consistency in hatred yet fully relented; hardly a generation since has not seen some Marini, or De Bonald, or Rallaye, or De Gabriac, suppressing evidence, or torturing expressions, or inventing theories, to blacken the memory of Galileo and save the reputation of the Church.[2]

---

[1] *Martin*, p. 243.

[2] For the persecution of Galileo's memory, see *Th. Martin*, chaps. ix and x. For documentary proofs, see *De l'Epinois*. For a collection of the slanderous theories invented against Galileo, see *Martin*, final chapters and appendix. Both these authors are devoted to the Church, but, unlike Monsignor Marini, are too upright to resort to the pious fraud of suppressing documents or interpolating pretended facts.

The action of the Church authorities corresponded well to the spirit thus exhibited; not until 1757, over one hundred years after his condemnation, was it removed, and then secretly; not until 1835, over two hundred years after his condemnation, was the record of it expunged from the *Index*.

But this is by no means the only important part of this history. Hardly less important, for one who wishes to understand the character of the warfare of science, is it to go back over those two hundred years between that fearful crime and its acknowledgment, and study the great retreat of the army of the Church after its disastrous victory over Galileo.

Having gained this victory, the conscientious believers in the Bible as a compendium of history and text-book of science exulted greatly. Loud was the rejoicing that the "heresy," the "infidelity," the " atheism," involved in believing that the earth revolves about its axis and moves around the sun, had been crushed by the great tribunal of the Church, acting in strict obedience to the expressed will of one pope and the written order of another.

But soon clear-sighted men saw that this victory was a disaster. From all sides came proofs that Kopernik and Galileo were right; and although Pope Urban and the Inquisition held Galileo in strict seclusion, not allowing him even to *speak* regarding the double motion of the earth; and although the condemnation of "all books which affirm the motion of the earth" was kept on the Index; and although the colleges and universities under Church control were compelled to teach the opposite doctrine, it was seen that the position gained by the victory over Galileo could not be maintained for ever. So began the great retreat —the retreat of the army of Church apologists through two centuries of sophistry, trickery, and falsehood.

The first important move in the retreat was a falling back upon the statement that Galileo was condemned, not because he affirmed the motion of the earth, but because he supported it from Scripture. For a considerable time this falsehood served its purpose; even a hundred and fifty years after Galileo's condemnation it was renewed by the Protestant Mallet du Pan,[1] in his wish to gain favor from the older Church; but the slightest critical examination of the original documents, recently revealed, show this position utterly untenable. The letters of Galileo to Castelli and the Grand-duchess Christine, in which he spoke of the Copernican theory as reconcilable with Scripture, were not published until after the condemnation; and although the Archbishop of Pisa had

[1] See *Martin*, pp. 401, 402.

endeavored to use them against him, they were but casually mentioned in 1616, and entirely left out of view in 1633. What was condemned in 1616 as "absurd, false in theology, and heretical, because absolutely contrary to Holy Scripture," was the proposition that "*the sun is the centre about which the earth revolves;*" and what was condemned as "absurd, false in philosophy, and, from a theologic point of view at least, opposed to the true faith," was the proposition that "*the earth is not the centre of the universe and immovable, but has a diurnal motion.*"[1]

What Galileo was made, by express order of Pope Urban and by the action of the Inquisition under threat of torture, to abjure, was "*the error and heresy of the movement of the earth.*"[2]

What the *Index*, prefaced by papal bulls binding its contents upon the consciences of the faithful, for two hundred years steadily condemned, were "*all books which affirm the motion of the earth.*"

Not one of these condemnations was directed against Galileo's private letters to Castelli and Christine affirming the possibility of reconciling his ideas to Scripture.

Having been dislodged from this point, the

[1] See *De l'Epinois*, p. 35, where the document is given in its original Latin.
[2] See translation of the abjuration in appendix to *Private Life of Galileo*, London, 1870.

Church apologists sought cover under the statement that "Galileo was condemned not for heresy, but for contumacy," and for "wanting in respect for the pope."[1]

As to the first point, the very language of the various sentences shows the falsehood of the assertion; they speak of "heresy," and never of "contumacy." As to the last point, the display of the original documents settled that forever. It was proved by them that from first to last he had been toward the pope most patient and submissive. He had indeed expressed his anger at times against his traducers; but to hold this the cause of the judgment against him, is to degrade the whole proceeding, and to convict the pope, Bellarmin, the theologians, and the Inquisition, of direct falsehood, since they assigned entirely different reasons for their conduct. From this, therefore, the apologists hastily retreated.

The next rally was made about the statement that the persecution of Galileo was the result of a quarrel between Aristotelian professors on one side and professors favoring the experimental method on the other, and that at first Pope Urban favored

---

[1] See *Marini*, who manipulated the original documents to prove this. Even Whewell appears to have been somewhat misled by him; but Whewell wrote before De l'Epinois had shown all the documents, and under the supposition that Marini was an honest man.

Galileo. But this position was attacked and carried by a very simple statement. If the Divine guidance of the Church is such a sham that it can be dragged into a professional squabble, and the pope made the tool of a faction in bringing about a most disastrous condemnation of a proven truth, how does the Church differ from any human organization sunk into decrepitude, managed by simpletons and controlled by schemers? If the argument be true, the condition of the Church is worse than its enemies have declared it. Amid the jeers of an unfeeling world the apologists sought new shelter.

The next point at which a stand was made was the assertion that the condemnation of Galileo was "provisory;" but this proved a more treacherous shelter than the other. When doctrines have been solemnly declared, as those of Galileo were solemnly declared, "contrary to the sacred Scriptures," "opposed to the true faith," and "false and absurd in theology and philosophy," to say that such declarations are "provisory,"[1] is to say that the truth held by the Church is not immutable; from this, then, the apologists retreated.

While this retreat was going on, there was a constant discharge of small-arms in the shape of innuendoes, hints, and small sophistries, by small

[1] See *Marini*.

writers; every effort was made to blacken Galileo's private character; the irregularities of his early life were dragged forth, and stress was laid on breaches of etiquette; but this succeeded so poorly, that in 1850 it was thought necessary by the Roman court to cover their retreat by some more careful strategy.

The original documents of the trial of Galileo had, during the storms of the early part of the century, been transferred to Paris; but after several years, in 1846, they were returned to Rome by the French government, on the express promise by the papal authorities that the decisions should be published. After various delays, on various pretexts, in 1850 the long-expected publication appeared. The ecclesiastic charged with presenting them to the world was Monsignor Marini. This ecclesiastic was of a kind which has too often afflicted the weary earth—fox-like in cunning, cat-like in treachery. Despite the solemn promise of the papal court, the wily Marini became the instrument of the Roman authority in evading the promise; by suppressing a document here, and interpolating a statement there, he managed to give plausible standing-ground for nearly every important sophistry ever broached to save the reputation of the Church and destroy the reputation of Galileo. He it was who supported the idea that "Galileo was condemned not for heresy, but for contumacy," and various other assertions as groundless.

The first effect of Monsignor Marini's book seemed favorable in covering the retreat of the Church; aided by him, such vigorous writers as Ward were able to throw up temporary intrenchments between the Church and the indignation of the world.

But some time later came an investigator very different from wily Monsignor Marini. This man was a Frenchman, M. de l'Epinois. Like Marini, De l'Epinois was devoted to the Church, but, unlike Marini, he could not lie. Having obtained access, in 1867, to the Galileo documents at the Vatican, he published fully all those of importance, without suppression or piously-fraudulent manipulation. This made all the intrenchments based upon Marini's statements untenable. Another retreat had to be made.

And now was made the most desperate effort of all. The apologistic army, reviving an idea which popes and Church had spurned, declared that the pope, *as pope*, had never condemned the doctrines of Kopernik and Galileo; that he had condemned them as a man simply; that therefore the Church had never been committed to them; that they were condemned by the cardinals of the Inquisition and Index, and that the pope had evidently been restrained from signing their condemnation by Providence.¹ Nothing could show the desperation of the retreating party better than jugglery like this. The facts are, that from Pope Urban downward, among the Church authorities of the seventeenth century, the decision was spoken of as made by the pope and the Church. Urban VIII. spoke of that of 1616 as made by Pope Paul V. and the Church, and of that of 1633 as made by himself and the Church.²

When Gassendi attempted to raise the point that the decision was not sanctioned by the Church as such, a great theological authority, Father Lecazre,³ rector of the College of Dijon, publicly contradicted him, and declared that it "was not certain cardinals, but the supreme authority of the Church," that had condemned Galileo; and to this statement the pope and the Church gave consent, either openly or by silence.³ The suspected thinkers, like Descartes and others, who attempted to raise the same point, were treated with contempt. Father Castelli, who had devoted himself to Galileo, and knew to his cost just what the condemnation meant and who made it, takes it for granted, in his letter to the papal authorities, that it was made by the Church. Cardinal Querenghi

---

¹ See *Epinois* and *Th. Martin, passim*.

² See pages 136, 144, and elsewhere in *Martin*, who, much against his will, is forced to allow this.

³ *Martin*, pp. 146, 147.

in his letters, the embassador Guicciardini in his dispatches, the historian Viviani in his biography of Galileo—all writing under Church inspection at the time—take the view that the Church condemned Galileo. The Inquisition itself, backed by the greatest theologian of the time, Bellarmin, took the same view;[1] and if this were not enough, we have the Roman Index, containing the condemnation for nearly two hundred years, prefaced by a solemn bull of the reigning pope, binding the condemnation on the consciences of the whole Church, and reiterating year after year the condemnation of "all books which affirm the motion of the earth" as damnable.[2] To attempt to face all this, added to the fact that the Inquisition condemned Galileo, and required his abjuration of "the heresy of the movement of the earth" by written order of the pope, was soon seen to be impossible.

In spite, then, of all the casuistry of De l'Epinois and all the special pleadings of M. Martin, the sturdy common-sense of the world proved too strong; and now comes to view the most astounding defense of all—that hinted at by Viscount de Bonald and developed in the *Dublin Review*. This was nothing less than an attempt to retreat under a charge of deception against the Almighty

[1] See Martin, p. 145.
[2] See note on condemnation of Kopernik.

himself. The argument is as follows: "But it may well be doubted whether the Church did retard the progress of scientific truth. What retarded it, was the circumstance that God has thought fit to express many texts of Scripture in words which have every appearance of denying the earth's motion. But it is God who did this, not the Church; and, moreover, since He thought fit so to act as to retard the progress of scientific truth, it would be little to her discredit even if it were true that she had followed His example."

With this, the retreat of the army of apologists is complete; further than this, through mazes of sophistry and into depths of contempt, they could not go.[1]

[1] For the attempt to make the crime of Galileo a breach of etiquette, see *Dublin Review*, as above. *Whewell*, vol. i., 393. Citation from *Marini:* "Galileo was punished for trifling with the authorities to which he refused to submit, and was punished for obstinate contumacy, not heresy." The sufficient answer to all this is, that the words of the inflexible sentence designating the condemned books are: "Libri omnes qui affirmant telluris motum." See *Bertrand*, p. 59. As to the idea that "Galileo was punished not for his opinion, but for basing it on Scripture," the answer may be found in the Roman Index of 1704, in which are noted for condemnation "Libri omnes docentes mobilitatem terræ et inmobilitatem solis." For the way in which, when it was found convenient in argument, Church apologists insisted that it *was* "the Supreme Chief of the Church, by a pontifical decree, and not certain cardinals," who condemned Galileo and his doctrine, see Father Lecazre's letter to Gassendi in *Flammarion, Pluralité des Mondes*, p. 427, and Urban VIII.'s own declarations as given

Do not understand me here as casting blame on the Roman Church at large. It must in fairness be said, that some of its best men tried to stop this great mistake. Even Pope Urban himself would have been glad at one time to stop it; but the current was too strong, and he weakly yielded, becoming a bitter persecutor.[1] The whole of the civilized world was at fault, Protestant as well as Catholic, and not any particular part of it. It was not the fault of religion; it was the fault of the short-sighted views which narrow-minded, loud-voiced men are ever prone to mix in with religion, and to insist are religion.[2]

by Martin. For the way in which, when necessary, Church apologists asserted the very contrary of this, declaring that "it was issued in a doctrinal decree of the Congregation of the Index, and *not* as the Holy Father's teaching," see *Dublin Review*, September, 1865. And for the most astounding attempt of all, to take the blame off the shoulders of both pope and cardinals, and place it upon the Almighty, see the article above cited, in the *Dublin Review*, September, 1865, p. 419. For a good summary of the various attempts, and for replies to them in a spirit of judicial fairness, see *Th. Martin, Vie de Galilée*, though there is some special pleading to save the infallibility of pope and Church. The bibliography at the close is very valuable.

[1] For Baronius's remark, see *De Morgan*, p. 26. Also, *Whewell*, vol. i., p. 394.

[2] For an exceedingly striking statement, by a Roman Catholic historian of genius, as to popular demand for persecution, and the pressure of the lower strata, in ecclesiastical organizations, for cruel measures, see *Balmès, Le Protestantisme comparé au Catholicisme*, etc., 4th ed., Paris, 1855, vol. ii. Archbishop Spaulding

But the losses to the earth in the long war against Galileo were followed by losses not less unfortunate in other quarters. There was then in Europe one of the greatest thinkers ever given to mankind—René Descartes. Mistaken though many of his theories were, they were fruitful in truths. The scientific warriors had stirred new life in him, and he was working over and summing up in his mighty mind all the researches of his time; the result must make an epoch in history. His aim was to combine all knowledge and thought into a "Treatise on the World." His earnestness he proved by the eleven years which he gave to the study of anatomy alone. Petty persecution he had met often, but the fate of Galileo robbed him of all hope, of all energy; the battle seemed lost; he gave up his great plan forever.[1]

But champions pressed on. Campanella, full of vagaries as he was, wrote his *Apologia pro Galileo*, though for that and other heresies, reli-

---

has something of the same sort in his Miscellanies. *L'Epinois, Galilée*, pp. 22, *et seq*., stretches this as far as possible, to save the reputation of the Church in the Galileo matter.

[1] *Humboldt, Cosmos*, London, 1851, vol. iii., p. 21. Also, *Lange, Geschichte des Materialismus*, vol. i., p. 222, where the letters of Descartes are given, showing his despair, and the giving up of his best thoughts and works to preserve peace with the Church. Also, *Saisset, Descartes et ses précurseurs*, pp. 100, *et seq.* Also, *Jolly, Hist. du Mouvement Intellectuel au XVIe Siècle*, vol. i., p. 390

gious and political, he seven times underwent torture.[1]

And Kepler comes. He leads science on to greater victories. Kopernik, great as he was, could not disentangle his scientific reasoning entirely from the theological bias. The doctrines of Aristotle and Thomas Aquinas as to the necessary superiority of the circle, had vitiated the minor features of his system, and left breaches in it through which the enemy was not slow to enter. Kepler sees these errors, and, by wonderful genius in insight and vigor in thought, he brings to the world the three laws which bear his name, and this fortress of science is complete. He thinks and speaks as one inspired. His battle is severe; he is sometimes abused, sometimes ridiculed, sometimes imprisoned. Protestants in Styria and at Tübingen, Catholics at Rome, press upon him;[2] but Newton, Halley, Bradley, and the other great leaders follow, and to science remains the victory.

[1] *Libri*, pp. 149, *et seq.*

[2] Fromundus, speaking of Kepler's explanation, says: "Vix teneo ebullientem risum." It is almost equal to the *New York Church Journal*, speaking of John Stuart Mill as "that small sciolist," and of the preface to Dr. Draper's recent work as "chippering." How a journal generally so fair in its treatment of such subjects can condescend to use such weapons, is one of the wonders of modern journalism. For Protestant persecution of Kepler, see vol. i., p. 392. Among other things, Kepler's mother was declared a witch, and this was followed by a reminder of the Scriptural injunction, "Ye shall not suffer a witch to live."

And yet the war did not wholly end. During the seventeenth century, in all France, after all the splendid proofs added by Kepler, no one dared openly teach the Copernican theory, and Cassini, the great astronomer, never declared it.[1] In 1672 Father Riccioli, a Jesuit, declared that there were precisely forty-nine arguments for the Copernican theory and seventy-seven against it; so that there remained twenty-eight reasons for preferring the orthodox theory.[2] Toward the end of the seventeenth century, after the demonstration of Sir Isaac Newton, even Bossuet, the "eagle of Meaux," among the loftiest of religious thinkers, declared for the Ptolemaic theory as the Scriptural theory;[3] and in 1724 John Hutchinson published in England his *Moses's Principia*, maintaining that the Hebrew Scriptures are a perfect system of natural philosophy, and are opposed to the Newtonian theory of gravitation.[4] In 1746 Boscovich, the great mathematician of the Jesuits, used these words: "As for me, full of respect for the Holy Scriptures and the decree of the Holy Inquisition, I regard the earth as immovable; nevertheless,

---

[1] For Cassini's position, see *Henri Martin, Hist. de France*, vol. xiii., p. 175.

[2] *Daunou, Études Historiques*, vol. ii., p. 439.

[3] Bossuet, see *Bertrand*, p. 41.

[4] For Hutchinson, see *Lyell, Principles of Geology*, Introduction.

for simplicity in explanation, I will argue as if the earth moves, for it is proved that of the two hypotheses the appearances favor that idea."[1] And even at a date far within our own nineteenth century, the authorities of the Spanish universities vigorously excluded the Newtonian system, and the greatest of them all, the University of Salamanca, held it under the ban until a very recent period.[2]

Nor has the opposition failed even in our own time. On the 5th of May, 1829, a great multitude assembled at Warsaw, to do honor to the memory of Kopernik, and to unveil Thorwaldsen's statue of him.

Kopernik had lived a pious, Christian life. He was well known for unostentatious Christian charity. With his religious belief no fault had ever been found; he was a canon of the church of

---

[1] Boscovich. This was in 1746, but in 1785 Boscovich seemed to feel his position in view of history, and apologized abjectly. *Bertrand*, pp. 60, 61. See also Whewell's notice of Le Sueur and Jacquier's introduction to their edition of *Newton's Principia*. For a clear statement of Bradley's exquisite demonstration of the Copernican theory by reasonings upon the rapidity of light, etc., and Foucault's exhibition of the rotation of the earth by the pendulum experiment, see *Hoefer, Hist. de l'Astronomie*, pp. 492, et. seq. For the most recent proofs of the Copernican theory, by discoveries of Bunsen, Bischoff, Benzenburg, and others, see *Jevons, Principles of Science*.

[2] See note in introduction to *Lyell's Principles of Geology;* also, *Buckle Hist. of Civ. in England*, vol. i., chap. i.

Frauenberg, and over his grave had been written the most touching of Christian epitaphs.

Naturally, then, the people expected a religious service. All was understood to be arranged for it. The procession marched to the church and waited. The hour passed, and no priest appeared; none could be induced to appear. Kopernik, simple, charitable, pious, one of the noblest gifts of God to the service of religion as well as science, was still held to be a reprobate. Five years after that, his book was still standing on the Index of books prohibited to Christians; and although, in 1757, under Benedict XIV., the Congregation of the Index had secretly allowed the ideas of Kopernik and Galileo to be simply tolerated, it was not until 1822, as we have seen, that Pius VII. allowed the publishing of them at Rome; and not until 1835 did the prohibition of them fully disappear from the Index.[1]

---

[1] *Bertrand, Fondateurs de l'Astron. Mod.*, p. 61. *Flammarion, Vie de Copernic*, chap. ix. As to the time when the decree of condemnation was repealed, various authorities differ. Artaud, p. 307, cited in an apologetic article in *Dublin Review*, September, 1865, says that Galileo's famous dialogue was published in 1744, at Padua, entire, and with the usual approbations. The same article also declares that in 1818 the ecclesiastical decrees were repealed by Pius VII., in full Consistory. Whewell says that Galileo's writings, after some opposition, were expunged from the *Index Expurgatorius* in 1818. Cantu, an authority rather favorable to the Church, says that Copernicus's work remained on the

The Protestantism of England was little better. In 1772 sailed the famous English expedition for scientific discovery under Cook. The greatest by far of all the scientific authorities chosen to accompany it was Dr. Priestley. Sir Joseph Banks had especially invited him; but the clergy of Oxford and Cambridge intervened. Priestley was considered unsound in his views of the Trinity; it was suspected that this would vitiate his astronomical observations; he was rejected, and the expedition crippled.[1]

Nor has the warfare against dead champions of science been carried on only by the older Church.

On the 10th of May, 1859, was buried Alexander von Humboldt. His labors were among the greatest glories of the century, and his funeral one of the most imposing that Berlin had ever seen; among those who honored themselves by their presence was the prince regent—the present emperor. But of the clergy it was observed that none were present save the officiating clergyman and a few regarded as unorthodox.[2]

Index as late as 1835. Cantu, *Histoire Universelle*, vol. xv., p. 483; and with this Th. Martin, not less favorable to the Church, but exceedingly careful as to the facts, agrees.

[1] See Weld, *History of the Royal Society*, vol. ii., p. 56, for the facts and the admirable letter of Priestley upon this rejection.

[2] *Bruhns* and *Lassell, Life of Humboldt*, London, 1873, vol. ii., p. 411.

Nor have attempts to renew the battle been wanting in these latter days. The attempt in the Church of England, in 1864, to fetter science, which was brought to ridicule by Herschel, Bowring, and De Morgan; the Lutheran assemblage at Berlin, in 1868, to protest against "science falsely so called," in the midst of which stood Pastor Knak denouncing the Copernican theory; the "Syllabus," the greatest mistake of the Roman Church, are all examples of this.[1]

And now, what has been won by either party in this long and terrible war? The party which would subordinate the methods and aims of science to those of theology, though in general obedient to deep convictions, had given to Christianity a series of the worst blows it had ever received. They had made large numbers of the best men in Europe hate it. Why did Ricetto and Bruno and Vanini, when the crucifix was presented to them in their hours of martyrdom, turn from that blessed image with loathing?[2] Simply because Christianity had been made to them identical with the most horrible oppression of the mind.

[1] For the very amusing details of the English attempt, and of the way in which it was met, see *De Morgan, Paradoxes*, p. 42. For Pastor Knak and his associates, see *Revue des Deux Mondes*, 1868.

[2] For a striking account, gathered from eye-witnesses of this frightful scene at the execution of Bruno, see letter of Scioppius in appendix to vol. iv. of *Libri, Hist. des Mathématiques*.

Worse than that, the well-meaning defenders of the faith had wrought into the very fibre of the European heart that most unfortunate of all ideas, the idea that there is a necessary antagonism between science and religion. Like the landsman who lashes himself to the anchor of the sinking ship, they had attached the fundamental doctrines of Christianity, by the strongest cords of logic which they could spin, to these mistaken ideas in science, and the advance of knowledge had wellnigh engulfed them.

On the other hand, what had science done for religion? Simply this: Kopernik, escaping persecution only by death; Giordano Bruno, burned alive as a monster of impiety; Galileo, imprisoned and humiliated as the worst of misbelievers; Kepler, hunted alike by Protestant and Catholic, had given to religion great new foundations, great new, ennobling conceptions, a great new revelation of the might of God.

Under the old system we have that princely astronomer, Alfonso of Castile, seeing the poverty of the Ptolemaic system, yet knowing no other, startling Europe with the blasphemy that if he had been present at creation he could have suggested a better ordering of the heavenly bodies. Under the new system you have Kepler, filled with a re ligious spirit, exclaiming, "I do think the thoughts of God." [1] The difference in religious spirit between these two men marks the conquest made in this, even by science, for religion.

But we cannot leave the subject of astronomy without noticing the most recent warfare. Especially interesting is it because at one period the battle seemed utterly lost, and then was won beautifully, thoroughly, by a legitimate advance in scientific knowledge. I speak of the Nebular Hypothesis.

The sacred writings of the Jews which we have inherited speak literally of the creation of the heavenly bodies by direct intervention, and for the convenience of the earth. This was the view of the Fathers of the Church, and was transmitted through the great doctors in theology.

More than that, it was crystallized in art. So have I seen, over the portal of the Cathedral of Freiburg, a representation of the Almighty making and placing numbers of wafer-like suns, moons, and stars; and at the centre of all, platter-like and largest of all, the earth.[2] The lines on the Creator's face show that He is obliged to contrive; the lines of his muscles show that He is obliged to toil.

---

[1] As a pendant to this ejaculation of Kepler may be cited those wondrous words of Linnæus: "Deum omnipotentem a tergo transeuntem vidi et obstupui."

[2] For papal bull representing the earth as a flat disk, see *Daunou, Études Historiques*, vol. ii., p. 421.

Naturally, then, did sculptors and painters of the mediæval and early modern period represent the Almighty as weary after labor, and enjoying dignified repose.

These ideas, more or less gross in their accompaniments, passed into the popular creed of the modern period.

But about the close of the last century, Bruno having guessed the fundamental fact of the nebular hypothesis, and Kant having reasoned out its foundation idea, Laplace developed it, showing the reason for supposing that our own solar system, in its sun, planets, satellites, with their various motions, distances, and magnitudes, is a natural result of the diminishing heat of a nebulous mass—a result obeying natural laws.

There was an outcry at once against the "atheism" of the scheme. The war raged fiercely. Laplace claimed that there were in the heavens many nebulous patches yet in the gaseous form, and pointed them out. He showed by laws of physics and mathematical demonstration that his hypothesis accounted in a most striking manner for the great body of facts, and, despite clamor, was gaining ground, when the improved telescopes resolved some of the patches of nebulous matter into multitudes of stars.

The opponents of the nebular hypothesis were overjoyed; they sang pæans to astronomy, because, as they said, it had proved the truth of Scripture. They had jumped to the conclusion that all nebulæ must be alike—that if *some* are made up of systems of stars, *all* must be so made up; that none can be masses of attenuated gaseous matter, because some are not.

Science, for a time, halted. The accepted doctrine became this: that the only reason why all the nebulæ are not resolved into distinct stars is because our telescopes are not sufficiently powerful. But in time came that wonderful discovery of the spectroscope and spectrum analysis, and this was supplemented by Fraunhofer's discovery that the spectrum of an ignited gaseous body is discontinuous, with interrupting lines; and this, in 1846, by Draper's discovery that the spectrum of an ignited solid is continuous, with no interrupting lines. And now the spectroscope was turned upon the nebulæ, and about one-third of them were found to be gaseous.

Again the nebular hypothesis comes forth stronger than ever. The beautiful experiment of Plateau on the rotation of a fluid globe comes in to strengthen if not to confirm it. But what was likely to be lost in this? Simply a poor conception of the universe. What to be gained? A far more worthy idea of that vast power which works in the universe, in all things by law, and in none by caprice.[1]

[1] For Bruno's conjecture (in 1591), see *Jevons*, vol. ii., p. 299.

CHEMISTRY AND PHYSICS.

The great series of battles to which I next turn with you were fought on those fields occupied by such sciences as Chemistry and Natural Philosophy.

Even before these sciences were out of their childhood, while yet they were tottering mainly toward childish objects and by childish steps, the champions of that same old mistaken conception of rigid Scriptural interpretation began the war. The catalogue of chemists and physicists persecuted or thwarted would fill volumes.

The first entrance of these sciences, as a well-

For Kant's part in the nebular hypothesis, see *Lange, Geschichte des Materialismus*, vol. i., p. 266. For value of Plateau's beautiful experiment very cautiously estimated, see *W. Stanley Jevons, Principles of Science*, London, 1874, vol. ii., p. 36. Also, *Elisée Réclus, The Earth*, translated by Woodward, vol. i., pp. 14–18, for an estimate still more careful. For a general account of discoveries of nature of nebulæ by spectroscope, see *Draper, Conflict between Religion and Science*. For a careful discussion regarding the spectra of solid, liquid, and gaseous bodies, see *Schellen, Spectrum Analysis*, pp. 100, et seq. For a very thorough discussion of the bearings of discoveries made by spectrum analysis upon the nebular hypothesis, ibid., pp. 532–537. For a presentation of the difficulties yet unsolved, see article by Plummer, in London *Popular Science Review* for January, 1875. For excellent short summary of recent observations and thought on this subject, see *T. Sterry Hunt, Address at the Priestley Centennial*, pp. 7, 8. For an interesting modification of this hypothesis, see Proctor's recent writings.

defined force, into the modern world, began in the thirteenth century. But the thirteenth century was marked by a revival of religious fervor; to this day the greatest and best works of the cathedral-builders are memorials of its depth and strength.

Out of this religious fervor naturally came a great growth of theological thought and ecclesiastical power, and the spirit of inquiry was soon obliged to take account of this influence.

First among the distinguished men who, in that century, laid foundations for modern science, was Albert of Bollstadt, better known as Albert the Great, the most renowned scholar of Germany.

Fettered though he was by the absurd methods of his time, led astray as he was by the scholastic spirit, he had conceived ideas of better methods and aims. His eye pierces the mists of scholasticism; he sees the light, and draws the world toward it. He stands among the great pioneers of modern physical and natural science. He aids in giving foundations to botany and chemistry, and Humboldt finds in his works the germ of the comprehensive science of physical geography.[1]

---

[1] For a very careful discussion of Albert's strength in investigation and weakness in yielding to scholastic authority, see *Kopp, Ansichten über die Aufgabe der Chemie von Geber bis Stahl, Braunschweig,* 1875, pp. 64, *et seq.* For a very extended and enthusiastic biographical sketch, see *Pouchet.* For comparison of his work

The conscience of the time, acting, as it supposed, in defense of religion, brought out a missile which it hurled with deadly effect. You see those mediæval scientific battle-fields strewed with such: it was the charge of sorcery, of unlawful compact with the devil.

This missile was effective. You find it used against every great investigator of Nature in those times and for centuries after. The list of great men charged with magic, as given by Naudé, is astounding. It includes every man of real mark, and the most thoughtful of the popes, Sylvester II. (Gerbert), stands in the midst of them. It seemed to be the received idea that, as soon as a man conceived a wish to study the works of God, his first step must be a league with the devil.[1]

This missile was hurled against Albert. He was condemned by the authorities of the Dominican order, subjected to suspicion and indignity, and only escaped persecution by yielding to the ecclesiastical spirit of the time, and working mainly in theological channels by scholastic methods. It was

with that of Thomas Aquinas, see *Milman, History of Latir Christians*, vol. vi., 461. *Il était aussi très-habile dans les arts mécaniques, ce que le fit soupçonner d'être sorcier.* Sprengel, *Histoire de la Médecine*, vol. ii., p. 389.

[1] For the charge of magic against scholars and others, see Naudé, *Apologie pour les grands hommes accusés de Magie, passim.* Also, *Maury, Hist. de la Magie*, troisième édit., pp. 214, 215. Also, Cuvier, *Hist. des Sciences Naturelles*, vol. i., p. 396.

a sad loss to the earth; and certainly, of all organizations that have reason to lament the pressure of those ecclesiastical forces which turned Albert the Great from the path of experimental philosophy, foremost of all in regret should be the Christian Church, and especially the Roman branch of it. Had the Church of the thirteenth century been so full of faith as to accept the truths in natural science brought by Albert and his compeers, and to have encouraged their growth, this faith and this encouragement would to this day have formed the greatest argument for proving the Church directly under Divine guidance; they would have been the brightest jewels in her crown. The loss to the Church, by this want of faith and courage, has proved, in the long-run, even greater than the loss to science.

The next great man of that age whom the theological and ecclesiastical forces of the time turn from the right path is Vincent of Beauvais.

Vincent devoted himself to the study of Nature in several of her most interesting fields. To astronomy, mineralogy, botany, and chemistry, he gave much thought; but especially did he devote himself to the preparation of a full account of the universe. Had he taken the path of experimental research, the world would have been enriched with most precious discoveries; but the impulse followed by Albert of Bollstadt, backed as it was by the whole ecclesiastical power of his time, was too strong, and, in all the life-labor of Vincent, nothing, appears of any permanent value. He built a structure which careless observation of facts, literal interpretation of Scripture, and theological subtilizing, combined to make one of the most striking monuments of human error.[1]

But the theological ecclesiastical spirit of the thirteenth century gained its greatest victory in the work of the most renowned of all thinkers of his time, St. Thomas Aquinas. In him was the theological spirit of his age incarnate. Although he yielded somewhat, at one period, to love of studies in natural science, it was he who finally made that great treaty or compromise which for ages subjected science entirely to theology. He it was whose thought reared the most enduring barrier against those who, in that age and in succeeding ages, labored to open for science the path by its own legitimate method toward its own noble ends.

Through the earlier systems of philosophy as they were then known, and through the earlier theologic thought, he had gone with great labor and vigor; he had been a pupil of Albert of Bollstadt, and from him had gained inspiration in science.

---

[1] See *Études sur Vincent de Beauvais par l'Abbé Bourgeat*, chaps. xii., xiii., xiv. Also, *Pouchet, Histoire des Sciences Naturelles au Moyen Age*, Paris, 1853, pp. 470, *et seq.*

All his mighty powers, thus disciplined and cultured, he brought to bear in making a treaty or truce, giving to theology the supremacy over science. The experimental method had already been practically initiated; Albert of Bollstadt and Roger Bacon had begun their work in accordance with its methods; but St. Thomas Aquinas gave all his thoughts to bringing science again under the sway of the theological bias, metaphysical methods, and ecclesiastical control. He gave to the world a striking example of what his method could be made to produce. In his commentary upon Aristotle's treatise upon "Heaven and Earth" he illustrates all the evils of such a combination of theological reasoning and literal interpretation of the Scriptural with scientific facts as then understood, and it remains to this day a prodigious monument to human genius and human folly. The ecclesiastical power of the time hailed him as a deliverer; it was claimed that striking miracles were vouchsafed, showing that the blessing of Heaven rested upon his labors. Among the legends embodying the Church spirit of that period is that given by the Bollandists and immortalized by a renowned painter. The great philosopher and saint is represented in the habit of his order, with book and pen in hand, kneeling before the image of Christ crucified; and as he kneels the image thus addresses him: "Thomas, thou hast written well concerning me; what price wilt thou receive for thy labor?" To this day the greater ecclesiastical historians of the Roman Church, like the Abbé Rohrbacher, and the minor historians of science, who find it convenient to propitiate the Church, like Pouchet, dilate upon the glories of St. Thomas Aquinas in thus making a treaty of alliance between religious and scientific thought, and laying the foundations for a "sanctified science." But the unprejudiced historian cannot indulge in this enthusiastic view. The results both for the Church and for the progress of science have been most unfortunate. It was a wretched step backward. The first result of this great man's great compromise was to close that new path in science which alone leads to discoveries of value—the experimental method—and to reopen the old path of mixed theology and science, which, as Hallam declares, "after three or four hundred years had not untied a single knot, or added one unequivocal truth to the domain of philosophy;" the path which, as all modern history proves, has ever since led only to delusion and evil.[1]

---

[1] For work of Aquinas, see *St. Thomas Aquinas, Liber de Cœlo et Mundo*, section xx. Also, *Life and Labors of St. Thomas of Aquin*, by *Archbishop Vaughan*, pp. 459, *et seq*. For his labors in natural science, see *Hoefer, Histoire de la Chimie*, Paris, 1843, vol. i., p. 381. For theological views of science in middle ages, and rejoicing thereat, see *Pouchet, Hist. des Sci. Nat. au Moyen Age*, *ubi supra*. Pouchet says: "En général au milieu du moyen Age

The path thus unfortunately opened by these strong men became the main path in science for ages, and it led the world farther and farther from any fruitful fact or hopeful method. Roger Bacon's investigations were virtually forgotten; worthless mixtures of literal interpretation of Scripture with imperfectly authenticated physical facts took their place.

Every age since has been full of examples of this, but out of them I will take just one; and it shall be no other than that Francis Bacon, who, more than any other man, led the modern world

les sciences sont essentiellement chrétiennes, leur but est tout-à-fait religieux, et elles semblent beaucoup moins s'inquiéter de l'avancement intellectuel de l'homme que de son salut eternel." Pouchet calls this "conciliation" into a "harmonieux ensemble" "la plus glorieuse des conquêtes intellectuelles du moyen age." Pouchet belongs to Rouen, and the shadow of the Rouen Cathedral seems thrown over all his history. See, also, *L'Abbé Rohrbacher, Hist. de l'Église Catholique*, Paris, 1858, vol. xviii., pp. 421, *et seq.* The abbé dilates upon the fact that "the Church organizes the agreement of all the sciences by the labors of St. Thomas of Aquin and his contemporaries." For the theological character of science in middle ages, recognized by a Protestant philosophic historian, see the well-known passage in *Guizot, History of Civilization in Europe;* and by a noted Protestant ecclesiastic, see *Bishop Hampden's Life of Thomas Aquinas*, chaps. xxxvi., xxxvii. See, also, *Hallam, Middle Ages*, chap. ix. For dealings of Pope John XXII., and kings of France and England, and republic of Venice, see *Figuier, L'Alchimie et les Alchimistes*, pp. 140, 141, where, in a note, the text of the bull *Spondent Pariter* is given.

out of the path opened by Aquinas, and back into the path trod by Roger Bacon. Strange as it may at first seem, Francis Bacon, whose keenness of sight revealed the delusions of the old path and the promises of the new, that man whose boldness in thought did so much to turn the world from the old path into the new, presents, in his own writings, one of the most striking examples of the strength of the evil he did so much to destroy.

The *Novum Organum*, considering the time when it came from his pen, is doubtless one of the greatest exhibitions of genius in the history of human thought. This treatise it was which showed the modern world the way out of the scholastic method and reverence for dogma into the experimental method and reverence for demonstrated fact. In the course of it occur many passages which show that the great philosopher was fully alive to the danger, both to religion and to science, arising from their mixture. Early in his argument he says: "But the corruption of philosophy from superstition and admixture of theology separates altogether more widely, and introduces the greatest amount of evil, both into whole systems of philosophy and into their parts." And a little later he says: "Some moderns have indulged this vanity with the greatest carelessness, and have endeavored to found a Natural Philosophy on the first of Genesis and the Book of Job, and other sacred Scriptures, so 'seeking the dead among the living.' And by so much the more is this vanity to be restrained and coerced because their expressions form an unwholesome mixture of things human and divine; not merely fantastic philosophy, but heretical religion. And so it is very salutary that, with due sobriety of mind, those things only be rendered to faith which are faith's."[1] Still later, in his treatise, Bacon returns to the charge yet more strongly. He says: "Nor is it to be overlooked, that natural philosophy has in all ages had a troublesome and stubborn adversary in superstition and the blind and immoderate zeal for religion. Thus it has been among the Greeks, that they who first proposed to the yet unprepared ears of men the natural causes of lightning and tempests were condemned, on that head, for impiety toward the gods; nor by some of the old fathers of the Christian religion were those much better received, who laid it down from the most sure demonstrations, such as no one in his senses could nowadays contradict, that the earth is round, and asserted in consequence that there must be antipodes. Furthermore, as things are now, the condition of discourses on Nature is made severe and more rigorous in consequence of the summaries and methods of scholastic theolo-

[1] The *Novum Organon*, translated by the Rev. G. W. Kitchin, Oxford, 1855, chap. lxv.

gians, who, while they have, as far as they could, reduced theology to order, and have fashioned it into the form of an art, have besides succeeded in mingling far more than was right of the quarrelsome and thorny philosophy of Aristotle with the body of religion."

"The fictions, too, of those who have not feared to deduce and confirm from the principles and authority of philosophies the true Christian religion, have the same tendency, though in a different way. These celebrated the wedding of faith and sense, as though it were lawful, with much pomp and solemnity, and soothed the minds of men with a grateful variety of things, but, meanwhile, mingled the divine with the human in ill-matched state. And in mixtures like this of theology with natural philosophy, those things only which are now received in philosophy are included; while novelties, though they be changes for the better, are all banished and driven out."

And, again, Bacon says: "Lastly you may find, thanks to the unskillfulness of some divines, the approach to any kind of philosophy, however improved, entirely closed up. Some, indeed, in their simplicity are rather afraid, lest perhaps a deeper inquiry into Nature should penetrate beyond the allowed limits of sobriety." Still further on Bacon penetrates into the very heart of the question in a vigorous way, and says: "Others, more craftily, conjecture and consider that, if the means be unknown, each single thing can be referred more easily to the hand and rod of God—a matter, as they think, of very great importance to religion: and this is nothing more nor less than wishing to *please God by a lie.*" And, finally, he says: "Whereas, if one considers the matter rightly, natural philosophy is, after God's word, the surest medicine for superstition, and also the most approved nourishment of faith." [1]

No man who has thought much upon the annals of his race can, without a feeling of awe, come into the presence of such inspired clearness of insight and boldness of utterance. The first thought of the reader is, that, of all men, this Francis Bacon is the most free from the unfortunate bias he condemns. He certainly cannot be deluded into the old path. But, as we go on through the treatise, we are surprised to find that the strong arm of Aquinas had been stretched over the intervening ages, and had laid hold upon this master-thinker of the sixteenth century. Only a few chapters further along we find Bacon, after alluding to the then recent voyage of Columbus, speaking of the prophecy of Daniel regarding the latter days, that "many shall run to and fro and knowledge be increased," as " clearly signifying that it is in

---

[1] *Novum Organon*, chap. lxxxix.

the fates, i. e., in providence, that the circumnavigation of the world, which through so many lengthy voyages seems to be entirely complete or in course of completion, and the increase of science, should happen in the same age."[1]

Here, then, we have this great man indulging in that very mixture of literal Scriptural interpretation and scientific thought which he had condemned, and therefrom evidently deducing the conclusion that these great voyages and discoveries, which were the beginning of a new world in thought and action, were the end of all things.

But in his great work on *The Advancement of Learning* the firm grip which the methods he condemned held upon him is shown yet more clearly. In his first book he shows how "that excellent Book of Job, if it be revolved with diligence, it will be found pregnant and swelling with natural philosophy," and endeavors to show that the "roundness of the world," the "fixing of the stars, ever standing at equal distance," the "depression of the southern pole," "matter of generation," and "matter of minerals," are "with great elegancy noted." But, curiously enough, he uses to support some of these truths the very texts which the Fathers of the Church used to destroy them, and those for which he finds Scriptural warrant most clearly are such as science

[1] *Novum Organon*, chap. xciii.

has since disproved. So, too, he says that Solomon was enabled by "donation of God" in his proverbs "to compile a natural history of all verdure."[1]

Certainly no more striking examples of the strength of the evil which he had all along been denouncing could be exhibited than these in his own writings; after this we cease to wonder at his blindness to the discoveries of Kopernik and the experiments of Gilbert.

I pass from the legions of those who from that day to this have stumbled into similar errors by degrading our sacred volume into a compendium of history or a text-book of science, and turn next to a far more serious class of effects arising from the great mediæval compromise between science and theology. We have considered the wrong road into which so many master-spirits were led or driven; we will now look at the war brought against those men of science who persevered in the right road.

The first great thinker who, in spite of some stumbling into theologic pitfalls, persevered in this true path was Roger Bacon. His life and works seem until recently to have been generally misunderstood. He has been ranked as a superstitious alchemist who stumbled upon some inven-

---

[1] *Bacon, The Advancement of Learning*, edited by W. Aldis Wright, London, 1873, pp. 47, 48.

tions; but more recent investigation has revealed him to be one of the great masters in human progress.

The advance of sound historical judgment seems likely to bring nearer to equality the fame of the two who bear the name of Bacon. Bacon of the chancellorship and the *Novum Organon* may not wane; but Bacon of the prison-cell and the *Opus Majus* steadily approaches him in brightness.[1]

More than three centuries before Francis Bacon advocated the experimental method, Roger Bacon practised it, and the results as now revealed are wonderful. He wrought with power in philosophy and in all sciences, and his knowledge was sound and exact. By him, more than by any other man of the middle ages, was the world put on the most fruitful paths of science— the paths which have led to the most precious inventions. Among them are clocks, lenses, burning specula, telescopes, which were given by him to the world, directly or indirectly. In his writings are found formulæ for extracting phosphorus, manganese, and bismuth. It is even claimed,

---

[1] For a very contemptuous statement of Lord Bacon's claim to his position as a philosopher, see *Lange, Geschichte des Materialismus*, Leipsic, 1874, vol. i., p. 219. For a more just statement, see *Brewster, Life of Sir Isaac Newton*. See, also, *Jevons, Principles of Science*, London, 1874, vol. ii., p. 298.

with much appearance of justice, that he investigated the power of steam. He seems to have very nearly reached also some of the principal doctrines of modern chemistry. But it should be borne in mind that his method of investigation was even greater than these vast results. In the age when metaphysical subtilizing was alone thought to give the title of scholar, he insisted on *real* reasoning and the aid of natural science by mathematics. In an age when experimenting was sure to cost a man his reputation, and was likely to cost him his life, he insisted on experiment and braved all its risks. Few greater men have lived. As we read the sketch given by Whewell of Bacon's process of reasoning regarding the refraction of light, he seems fairly inspired.[1]

On this man came the brunt of the battle. The most conscientious men of his time thought it their duty to fight him, and they did it too well. It was not that he disbelieved in Christianity; *that* was never charged against him. His orthodoxy was perfect. He was attacked and condemned, in the words of his opponents, "*propter quasdam novitates suspectas.*"

He was attacked, first of all, with that goodly

[1] Kopp, in his *Ansichten*, pushes criticism even to some skepticism as to Roger Bacon being the *discoverer* of many of the things generally attributed to him; but, after all deductions are carefully made, enough remains to make Bacon the greatest benefactor to humanity during the middle ages.

old missile, which, with the epithets "infidel" and "atheist," has decided the fate of so many battles—the charge of magic and compact with Satan.

He defended himself with a most unfortunate weapon—a weapon which exploded in his hands and injured him more than the enemy, for he argued against the idea of compacts with Satan, and showed that much which is ascribed to demons results from natural means. This added fuel to the flame. To limit the power of Satan was deemed hardly less impious than to limit the power of God.[1]

The most powerful protectors availed him little. His friend Guy Foulkes having been made pope, Bacon was for a time shielded, but the fury of the enemy was too strong. In an unpublished letter, Blackstone declares that when, on one occasion, Bacon was about to perform a few experiments for some friends, all Oxford was in an uproar. It was believed that Satan was let loose. Everywhere were priests, fellows, and students rushing about, their garments streaming in the wind, and everywhere resounded the cry, "Down with conjurer!" and this cry, "Down with the conjurer!" resounded from cell to cell and hall to hall.[2]

---

[1] For an account of Bacon's treatise, *De Nullitate Magiæ*, see Hoefer.

[2] *Kopp, Geschichte der Chemie*, Braunschweig, 1843, vol. i., p. 68;

But the attack took a shape far more terrible. The two great religious orders, Franciscan and Dominican, vied with each other in fighting the new thought in chemistry and philosophy. St. Dominic, sincere as he was, solemnly condemned research by experiment and observation. The general of the Franciscan order took similar grounds.

In 1243 the Dominicans solemnly interdicted every member of their order from the study of medicine and natural philosophy, and in 1287 this interdiction was extended to the study of chemistry.[1] In 1278 the authorities of the Fran-

---

and for a somewhat reactionary discussion of Bacon's relation to the progress of chemistry, see a recent work by the same author, *Ansichten über die Aufgabe der Chemie*, Braunschweig, 1874, pp. 85, *et seq.* Also, for an excellent summary, see *Hoefer, Hist. de la Chimie*, vol. i., pp. 368, *et seq.* For summaries of his work in other fields, see *Whewell*, vol. i., pp. 367, 368. *Draper*, p. 438. *Saisset, Descartes et ses Précurseurs*, deuxième édition, pp. 397, *et seq.* *Nourrisson, Progrès de la pensée humaine*, pp. 271, 272. *Sprengel, Histoire de la Médecine*, Paris, 1865, vol. ii., p. 397. *Cuvier, Histoire des Sciences Naturelles*, vol. i., p. 417. As to Bacon's orthodoxy, see *Saisset*, pp. 53, 55. For special examination of causes of Bacon's condemnation, see *Waddington*, cited by Saisset, p. 14. On Bacon as a sorcerer, see Featherstonaugh's article in *North American Review*. For a good example of the danger of denying full power of Satan, even in much more recent times, and in a Protestant country, see account of treatment of *Bekker's Monde Enchanté* by the theologians of Holland, in *Nisard, Histoire des Livres Populaires*, vol. i., pp. 172, 173.

[1] *Henri Martin, Hist. de France*, vol. iv., p. 283.

ciscan order, assembled at Paris, solemnly condemned Bacon's teachings.

Another weapon began to be used upon the battle-fields of that time with much effect. The Arabs had made noble discoveries in science. Averroes had, among many, divided the honors with St. Thomas Aquinas. These facts gave the new missile: it was the epithet "Mahometan." This, too, was flung with effect at Bacon.[1]

Bacon was at last conquered. He was imprisoned for fourteen years. At the age of eighty years he was released from prison, but death alone took him beyond the reach of his enemies. How deeply the struggle had racked his mind may be gathered from that last affecting declaration of his: "Would that I had not given myself so much trouble for the love of science!"

Sad is it to think of what this great man might have given to the world had the world not refused the gift. He held the key of treasures which would have freed mankind from ages of error and misery. With his discoveries as a basis, with his method as a guide, what might not the world have gained! Nor was the wrong done to that age alone; it was done to this age also. The nineteenth century was robbed at the same time with the thirteenth. But for that interfer-

---

[1] On Bacon as a "Mahometan," see *Saisset*, p. 17.

ence with science, the nineteenth century would, without doubt, be enjoying discoveries which will not be reached before the twentieth century. Thousands of precious lives shall be lost in this century, tens of thousands shall suffer discomfort, privation, sickness, poverty, ignorance, for lack of discoveries and methods which, but for this mistaken religious fight against Bacon and his compeers, would now be blessing the earth.

In 1868 and 1869, sixty thousand children died in England and in Wales of scarlet fever; probably nearly as many died in this country. Had not Bacon been hindered, we should have had in our hands, by this time, the means to save two-thirds of these victims; and the same is true of typhoid, typhus, and that great class of diseases of whose physical causes science is just beginning to get an inkling. Put together all the efforts of all the atheists who have ever lived, and they have not done so much harm to Christianity and the world as has been done by the narrow-minded, conscientious men who persecuted Roger Bacon, and closed the path which he gave his life to open.[1]

---

[1] For proofs that the world is steadily working toward great discoveries as to the cause and prevention of zymotic diseases and of their propagation, see *Beale's Disease Germs*, *Baldwin Latham's Sanitary Engineering*, *Michel Lévy, Traité d'Hygiène Publique et Privée*, Paris, 1869. And for very thorough summaries, see President Barnard's paper read before Sanitary Congress

But, despite the persecution of Bacon and the defection of those who ought to have followed him, champions of natural science and the experimental method arose from time to time during the succeeding centuries. We know little of them personally. Our main knowledge of their efforts is derived from the efforts of their opponents and persecutors.

In 1317 Pope John XXII. issued his bull *Spondent Pariter*, nominally leveled at the alchemists, but really dealing a terrible blow at the beginnings of the science of chemistry.

In 1380 Charles V. of France carried out the same policy, and even forbade the possession of furnaces and apparatus necessary for chemical processes. Under this law the chemist John Barillon, for possessing chemical furnaces and apparatus, was thrown into prison, and it was only by the greatest effort that his life was saved.

In 1404 Henry IV. of England issued a decree of the same sort; and in 1418 the republic of Venice followed the example of pope and kings. But champions of science still pressed on. Antonio de Dominis relinquishes his archbishopric of Spalatro, investigates the phenomena of light, and dies in the clutches of the Inquisition.[1]

in New York, 1874, and *Dr. J. C. Dalton's Anniversary Discourse on the Origin and Propagation of Disease*, New York, 1874.

[1] Antonio de Dominis, see *Montucla, Hist. des Mathématiques*, vol. i., p. 705. *Humboldt, Cosmos. Libri*, vol. iv., pp. 145, *et seq.*

Pierre de la Ramée stands up against Aristotelianism at Paris. A royal edict, sought by the Church, stopped his teaching, and the massacre of St. Bartholomew ended his life.

Somewhat later, John Baptist Porta began his investigations. Despite many absurdities, his work was most fruitful. His book on meteorology was the first in which sound ideas were broached. His researches in optics gave the world the camera obscura, and, possibly, the telescope. In chemistry he seems to have been the first to show how to reduce the metallic oxides, and thus to have laid the foundation of all those industries based upon the staining and coloring of glass and enamels; and, last of all, he did much to change natural philosophy from a "black art" to a vigorous open science. He encountered the same old policy of conscientious men. The society founded by him for physical research, "I Secreti," was broken up, and he was summoned to Rome and censured.[1]

In 1624 some young chemists of Paris, having taught the experimental method and cut loose from Aristotle, the Faculty of Theology besets the Parliament of Paris, and the Parliament prohibits this new chemical teaching under penalty of death.[2]

---

[1] For Porta, see *Hoefer, Hist. de la Chemie*, vol. ii., pp. 102–106. Also, *Kopp*. Also, *Sprengel, Hist de la Médecine*, iii., p. 239. Also, *Musset-Parthay*.

[2] *Henri Martin, Histoire de France*, vol. xii., pp. 14, 15.

The war went on in Italy. In 1657 occurred the first sitting of the *Accademia del Cimento*, at Florence, under the presidency of Prince Leopold dei Medici. This Academy promised great things for science. It was open to all talent. Its only fundamental law was "the repudiation of any favorite system or sect of philosophy, and the obligation to investigate Nature by the pure light of experiment."

The new Academy entered into scientific investigations with energy; Borelli in mathematics, Redi in natural history, and many others, pushed on the boundaries of knowledge. Heat, light, magnetism, electricity, projectiles, digestion, the incompressibility of water, were studied by the right method and with results that enriched the world.

The Academy was a fortress of science, and siege was soon laid to it. The votaries of scholastic learning denounced it as irreligious. Quarrels were fomented. Leopold was bribed with a cardinal's hat and drawn away to Rome; and, after ten years of beleaguering, the fortress fell: Borelli was left a beggar; Oliva killed himself in despair.[1]

Napier, Florentine History, vol. v., p. 485. *Tiraboschi, Storia della Literatura*. *Henri Martin, Histoire de France*. *Jevons Principles of Science*, vol. ii., pp. 36-40. For value attached to Borelli's investigations by Newton and Huyghens, see *Brewster's*

Still later, just before the great discoveries by Stahl, we find his predecessor Becher opposed with the following syllogism: "King Solomon, according to the Scriptures, possessed the united wisdom of heaven and earth. But King Solomen sent his vessels to Ophir to seek gold, and he levied taxes upon his subjects. Now, if Solomon had known anything about alchemy, he would not have done this; therefore Solomon did not know anything about alchemy (or chemistry in the form which then existed); therefore alchemy (or chemistry) has no reality or truth." And we find that Becher is absolutely turned away from his labors, and obliged to devote himself to proving that Solomon used more money than he possibly could have obtained from Ophir or his subjects, and therefore that he must have possessed a knowledge of chemical methods and the philosopher's stone as the result of them.[1]

And, in our time, Joseph de Maistre, uttering his hatred of physical sciences, declaring that man

Life of Sir Isaac Newton, London, 1875, pp. 128, 129. Libri, in his *Essai sur Galilée*, p. 37, says that Oliva was summoned to Rome, and so tortured by the Inquisition that, to escape further cruelty, he ended his life by throwing himself from a window.

[1] For this syllogism, see *Figuier, L'Alchimie et les Alchimistes*, pp. 106, 107. For careful appreciation of Becher's position in the history of chemistry, see *Kopp, Ansichten über die Aufgabe der Chemie*, etc., *von Geber bis Stahl*, Braunschweig, 1875, pp. 201, *et seq.*

has paid too dearly for them, asserting that they must be subjected to theology, likening them to fire—good when confined, but fearful when scattered about—this brilliant thinker has been the centre of a great opposing camp, an army of good men who cannot relinquish the idea that the Bible is a text-book of science.

ANATOMY AND MEDICINE.

I pass, now, to fields of more immediate importance to us—to anatomy and medicine.

It might be supposed that the votaries of sciences like these would be suffered to escape attack; unfortunately, they have had to stand in the thickest of the battle.

The Church, even in its earliest centuries, seems to have developed a distrust of them. Tertullian, in his "Treatise upon the Soul," stigmatizes the surgeon Herophilus as a "butcher," and evidently on account of his skill in his profession rather than on account of his want of it. St. Augustine, in his great treatise on the City of God, which remains to this day one of the treasures of the Church, speaks with some bitterness of "medical men who are called anatomists," and says that "with a cruel zeal for science they have dissected the bodies of the dead, and sometimes of sick persons, who have died under their knives, and have inhumanly pried into the secrets of the human body to learn the nature of disease and its exact seat, and how it might be cured!" [1]

But it was not until the mixture of theology and science had begun to ferment, in the thirteenth century, and the ecclesiastical power had been aroused in behalf of this sacred mixture, that the feeling against medical science broke into open war. About the beginning of that century Pope Innocent III. forbade surgical operations by priests, deacons, or subdeacons. Pope Honorius went still further, and forbade medicine to be practised by archdeacons, priests, or deacons; in 1243 the Dominican authorities banished books on medicine from their monasteries; somewhat later, Pope Boniface VIII. interdicted dissection as sacrilege.[2]

[1] For Tertullian's views, see the *De Anima*, chap. x. For views of St. Augustine, see the *De Civ. Dei*, book xxii., chap. 24.

[2] For Boniface VIII. and his interdiction of dissections, see *Buckle's Posthumous Works*, vol. ii., p. 567. For injurious effects of this ecclesiastical hostility to anatomy upon the development of art, see *Woltman, Holbein and His Time*, pp. 266, 267. For an excellent statement of the true relation of the medical profession to religious questions, see *Prof. Acland, General Relations of Medicine in Modern Times*, Oxford, 1868. For thoughtful and witty remarks on the struggle at a recent period, see *Maury, L'Ancienne Académie des Sciences*, Paris, 1864, p. 148. Maury says: "La faculté n'aimait pas à avoir affaire aux théologiens qui procèdent par anathèmes beaucoup plus que par analyses."

Toward the close of that great religious century came a battle which serves to show the spirit of the time.

The great physician and chemist of the day was Arnold de Villa Nova. Although he has been overrated by some modern historians as a votary of the experimental method, and underrated by others as a votary of alchemy, the sober judgment of the most thoughtful has acknowledged him as one of the most useful forerunners of modern masters in medical and chemical science.

The missile usual in such cases was hurled at him. He was charged with sorcery and dealings with the devil. The Archbishop of Tarragona first excommunicated him and drove him from Spain; next he was driven from Paris, and took refuge at Montpellier; thence, too, he was driven, finally, every place in France was closed against him, and he became an outcast.[1]

Such seemed the fate of men in that field who

[1] For uncritical praise of Arnold de Villa Nova, see *Figuier, L'Alchimie et les Alchimistes*, 3ème edit. For undue blame, see *Hoefer, Histoire de la Chimie*, Paris, 1842, vol. i., p. 386. For a more broad and fair judgment, see *Kopp, Geschichte der Chemie*, Braunschweig, 1843, vol. i., p. 66, and vol. ii., p. 185. Also, *Pouchet, Histoire des Sciences Naturelles au Moyen Age*, Paris, 1853, pp. 52, et seq. Also, *Draper, Int. Dev. of Europe*, p. 421. *Whewell, Hist. of the Induct. Sciences*, vol. i., p. 235; vol. viii., p. 86. *Frédault, Hist. de la Médecine*, vol. i., p. 204.

gained even a glimmer of new scientific truth. Even men like Cardan, and Paracelsus, and Porta, who yielded much to popular superstitions, were at once set upon if they ventured upon any other than the path which the Church thought sound—the insufficient path of Aristotelian investigation.

We have seen that the weapons used against the astronomers were mainly the epithets "infidel" and "atheist." We have also seen that the missiles used against the chemists and physicians were the epithets "sorcerer" and "leaguer with the devil," and we have picked up on various battle-fields another effective weapon, the epithet "Mohammedan."

On the heads of the anatomists and physicians were concentrated *all* these missiles. The charge of atheism ripened into a proverb: "*Ubi sunt tres medici, ibi sunt duo athei.*" Magic seemed so common a charge that many of the physicians seemed to believe it themselves. Mohammedanism and Averroism became almost synonymous with medicine, and Petrarch stigmatized Averroists as "men who deny Genesis and bark at Christ."[1]

Not to weary you with the details of earlier

---

[1] *Renan, Averroès et l'Averroisme*, Paris, 1867, pp. 327, 333, 335. For a perfectly just statement of the only circumstances which can justify the charge of "atheism," see Dr. Deems's article in POPULAR SCIENCE MONTHLY, February, 1876.

struggles, I will select a great benefactor of mankind and champion of scientific truth at the period of the revival of learning and the Reformation—Andreas Vesalius, the founder of the modern science of anatomy. The battle waged by this man is one of the glories of our race.

The old methods were soon exhausted by his early fervor, and he sought to advance science by truly scientific means—by patient investigation and by careful recording of results.

From the outset Vesalius proved himself a master. In the search for real knowledge he braved the most terrible dangers. Before his time the dissection of the human subject was thought akin to sacrilege. Occasionally an anatomist, like Mundinus, had given some little display with such a subject; but, for the purposes of *investigation*, such dissection was forbidden.[1] As we have already seen, even such men in the early Church as Tertullian and St. Augustine held anatomy in

---

[1] *Whewell*, vol. iii., p. 328, says, rather loosely, that Mundinus "dissected at Bologna in 1315." How different his idea of dissection was from that introduced by Vesalius, may be seen by Cuvier's careful statement that the entire number of dissections by Mundinus was three. The usual statement is that it was two. See *Cuvier, Hist. des Sci. Nat.*, tome iii., p. 7; also, *Sprengel, Frédault,* and *Hallam;* also, *Littré, Médecine et Médecins,* chap. on anatomy. For a very full statement of the agency of Mundinus in the progress of anatomy, see *Portal, Hist. de l'Anatomie et de la Chirurgérie,* vol. i., pp. 209-216

abhorrence, and Boniface VIII. interdicted dissection as sacrilege.

Through this sacred conventionalism Vesalius broke without fear. Braving ecclesiastical censure and popular fury, he studied his science by the only method that could give useful results. No peril daunted him. To secure the material for his investigations, he haunted gibbets and charnel-houses; in this search he risked alike the fires of the Inquisition and the virus of the plague. First of all men he began to place the science of human anatomy on its solid, modern foundations —on careful examination and observation of the human body. This was his first great sin, and it was soon aggravated by one considered even greater.

Perhaps the most unfortunate thing that has ever been done for Christianity is the tying it to forms of science which are doomed and gradually sinking. Just as, in the time of Roger Bacon, excellent but mistaken men devoted all their energies to binding Christianity to Aristotle; just as, in the time of Reuchlin and Erasmus, they insisted on binding Christianity to Thomas Aquinas: so, in the time of Vesalius, such men made every effort to link Christianity to Galen.

The cry has been the same in all ages; it is the same which we hear in this age for curbing scientific studies—the cry for what is called " sound learning." Whether standing for Aristotle against Bacon, or Aquinas against Erasmus, or Galen against Vesalius, or making mechanical Greek verses at Eton instead of studying the handiwork of the Almighty, or reading Euripides with translations instead of Lessing and Goethe in the original, the cry always is for "sound learning." The idea always is that these studies are *safe*.

At twenty-eight years of age Vesalius gave to the world his great work on human anatomy. With it ended the old and began the new. Its researches, by their thoroughness, were a triumph of science; its illustrations, by their fidelity, were a triumph of art.

To shield himself, as far as possible, in the battle which he foresaw must come, Vesalius prefaced the work by a dedication to the Emperor Charles V. In this dedicatory preface he argues for his method, and against the parrot repetitions of the mediæval text-books; he also condemns the wretched anatomical preparations and specimens made by physicians who utterly refused to advance beyond the ancient master.

The parrot-like repeaters of Galen gave battle at once. After the manner of their time, their first missiles were epithets; and, the almost infinite magazine of these having been exhausted, they began to use sharper weapons—weapons theologic.

At first the theologic weapons failed. A conference of divines having been asked to decide whether dissection of the human body is sacrilege, gave a decision in the negative. The reason is simple: Charles V. had made Vesalius his physician, and could not spare him. But, on the accession of Philip II. of Spain, the whole scene changed. That most bitter of bigots must of course detest the great innovator.

A new weapon was now forged. Vesalius was charged with dissecting living men,[1] and, either from direct persecution, as the great majority of authors assert, or from indirect influences, as the recent apologists for Philip II. allow, Vesalius became a wanderer. On a pilgrimage to the Holy Land to atone for his sin, he was shipwrecked, and in the prime of his life and strength he was lost to this world.

And yet not lost. In this century he again stands on earth; the painter Hamann has again given him to us. By the magic of Hamann's pencil, we look once more into Vesalius's cell. Its windows and doors, bolted and barred within, betoken the storm of bigotry which rages without; the crucifix, toward which he turns his eyes, symbolizes the spirit in which he labors; the corpse

---

[1] For a similar charge against anatomical investigations at a much earlier period, see *Littré, Médecine et Médecins*, chapter on anatomy.

of the plague-stricken, over which he bends, ceases to be repulsive; his very soul seems to send forth rays from the canvas which strengthen us for the good fight in this age.[1]

He was hunted to death by men who conscientiously supposed he was injuring religion. His poor, blind foes destroyed one of religion's greatest apostles. What was his influence on religion? He substituted for repetition, by rote, of worn-out theories of dead men, conscientious and reverent searching into the works of the living God; he substituted for representations of the human structure—pitiful and unreal—truthful representations, revealing the Creator's power and goodness in every line.[2]

I hasten now to the most singular struggle and victory of medical science between the sixteenth and nineteenth centuries.

Early in the last century, Boyer presented Inoculation as a preventive of small-pox, in France; thoughtful physicians in England, led by Lady Montagu and Maitland, followed his example.

---

[1] The original painting of Vesalius at work in his cell, by Hamann, is now at Cornell University.

[2] For a curious example of weapons drawn from Galen and used against Vesalius, see *Lewes, Life of Goethe*, p. 343, note. For proofs that I have not over-estimated Vesalius, see *Portal, ubi supra*. Portal speaks of him as "*le génie le plus droit qu'eut l'Europe;*" and again, "*Vesale me paraît un des plus grands hommes qui ait existé.*"

Theology took fright at once on both sides of the Channel. The French theologians of the Sorbonne solemnly condemned the practice. English theologians were most loudly represented by the Rev. Edward Massy, who, in 1722, preached a sermon in which he declared that Job's distemper was probably confluent small-pox, and that he had been doubtless inoculated by the devil; that diseases are sent by Providence for the punishment of sin, and that the proposed attempt to prevent them is "a diabolical operation." This sermon was entitled "The Dangerous and Sinful Practice of Inoculation." Not less absurd was the sermon of the Rev. Mr. Delafaye, entitled "Inoculation an Indefensible Practice." Thirty years later the struggle was still going on. It is a pleasure to note one great churchman, Maddox, Bishop of Worcester, giving battle on the side of right reason; but as late as 1753 we have the Rector of Canterbury denouncing inoculation from his pulpit in the primatial city, and many of his brethren following his example. Among the most common weapons hurled by churchmen at the supporters of inoculation, during all this long war, were charges of sorcery and atheism.[1]

[1] See *Sprengel, Histoire de la Médecine*, vol. vi., pp. 39–80. For the opposition of the Paris Faculty of Theology to inoculation, see the *Journal de Barbier*, vol. vi., p. 294. For bitter denunciations of inoculation by the English clergy, and for the noble

Nor did Jenner's blessed discovery of vaccination escape opposition on similar grounds. In 1798 an anti-vaccine society was formed by clergymen and physicians, calling on the people of England to suppress vaccination as "bidding defiance to Heaven itself—even to the will of God," and declaring that "the law of God prohibits the practice." In 1803 the Rev. Dr. Ramsden thundered against it in a sermon before the University of Cambridge, mingling texts of Scripture with calumnies against Jenner; but Plumptre in England, Waterhouse in America, and a host of other good men and true, press forward to Jenner's side, and at last science, humanity, and right reason, gain the victory.[1]

But I pass to one typical conflict in our days. In 1847 James Young Simpson, a Scotch physician of eminence, advocated the use of anæsthetics in obstetrical cases.

Immediately a storm arose. From pulpit after pulpit such a use of chloroform was denounced as

stand against them by Maddox, see *Baron, Life of Jenner*, vol. i., pp. 231, 232, and vol. ii., pp. 39, 40. For the strenuous opposition of the same clergy, see *Weld, History of the Royal Society*, vol. i., p. 464, note. Also, for the comical side of this matter, see *Nichols's Literary Illustrations*, vol. v., p. 800.

[1] For the opposition of conscientious men in England to vaccination, see *Duns, Life of Sir James Y. Simpson, Bart.*, London, 1873, pp. 248, 249; also, *Baron, Life of Jenner, ubi supra*, and vol. ii., p. 43; also, *Works of Sir J. Y. Simpson*, vol. ii.

impious. It was declared contrary to Holy Writ, and texts were cited abundantly. The ordinary declaration was, that to use chloroform was " to avoid one part of the primeval curse on woman." [1]

Simpson wrote pamphlet after pamphlet to defend the blessing which he brought into use; but the battle seemed about to be lost, when he seized a new weapon. "My opponents forget," said he, "the twenty-first verse of the second chapter of Genesis. That is the record of the first surgical operation ever performed, and that text proves that the Maker of the universe, before he took the rib from Adam's side for the creation of Eve, caused a deep sleep to fall on Adam."

This was a stunning blow; but it did not entirely kill the opposition. They had strength left to maintain that "the deep sleep of Adam took place before the introduction of pain into the world—in the state of innocence." [2] But now a new champion intervened — Thomas Chalmers. With a few pungent arguments he scattered the enemy forever, and the greatest battle of science against suffering was won. [3]

But was not the victory won also for religion? Go to yonder monument, in Boston, to one of the discoverers of anæsthesia. Read this inscription

---

[1] See *Duns, Life of Sir J. Y. Simpson*, pp. 215-222.
[2] *Ibid.*, pp. 256-259.
[3] *Ibid.*, p. 260; also, *Works of Sir J. Y. Simpson, ubi supra.*

from our sacred volume: "This also cometh from the Lord of hosts, which is wonderful in counsel and excellent in working."

GEOLOGY.

I now ask you to look at another part of the great warfare, and I select it because it shows more clearly than any other how Protestant nations, and in our own time, have suffered themselves to be led into the same errors that have wrought injury to religion and science in other times. We will look very briefly at the battle-fields of Geology.

From the first lispings of this science there was war. The prevailing doctrine of the Church was, that "in the beginning God made the heavens and the earth;" that "all things were made at the beginning of the world;" and that to say that stones and fossils have been made since "the beginning," is contrary to Scripture. The theological substitutes for scientific explanations ripened into such as these: that the fossils are "sports of Nature," or "creations of plastic force," or "results of a seminal air acting upon rocks," or "models" made by the Creator before he had fully decided upon the best manner of creating various beings. But, while some latitude was allowed among these theologico-scientific explanations, it was held essential to believe that they were placed in all the strata, on one of the creation-days, by the hand of the Almighty; and that this was done for some mysterious purpose of his own, probably for the trial of human faith.

In the sixteenth century Fracastoro and Palissy broached the true idea, but produced little effect. Near the beginning of the seventeenth century De Clave, Bitaud, and De Villon revived it; straightway the theologic faculty of Paris protested against the doctrine as unscriptural, destroyed the offending treatises, banished the authors from Paris, and forbade them to live in towns or enter places of public resort.[1] At the middle of the eighteenth century, Buffon made another attempt to state simple and fundamental geological truths. The theological faculty of the Sorbonne immediately dragged him from his high position, forced him to recant ignominiously, and to print his recantation. It required a hundred and fifty years for science to carry the day fairly against this single preposterous theory. The champion who dealt it the deadly blow was Scilla, and his weapons were facts revealed by the fossils of Calabria.

But the advocates of tampering with scientific reasoning now retired to a new position. It was strong, for it was apparently based on Scripture,

---

[1] *Morley, Life of Palissy the Potter*, vol. ii., pp. 315, *et seq.*

though, as the whole world now knows, an utterly false interpretation of Scripture. The new position was, that the fossils were produced by the Deluge of Noah.

In vain had it been shown, by such devoted Christians as Bernard Palissy, that this theory was utterly untenable; in vain did good men protest against the injury sure to result to religion by tying it to a scientific theory sure to be exploded: the doctrine that fossils were the remains of animals drowned at the flood continued to be upheld by the great majority as "sound doctrine," and as a blessed means of reconciling science with Scripture.[1]

To sustain this "Scriptural view," so called, efforts were put forth absolutely herculean, both by Catholics and Protestants. Mazurier declared certain fossil remains of a mammoth, discovered in France, to be bones of giants mentioned in Scripture. Father Torrubia did the same thing in Spain. Increase Mather sent similar remains, discovered in America, to England, with a similar statement. Scheuchzer made parade of the bones of a great lizard discovered in Germany, as the *homo diluvii testis*, the fossil man, proving the reality of the Deluge.[2]

---

[1] *Audial, Vie de Palissy*, p. 412. *Cantu, Hist. Universelle*, vol. xv., p. 492.

[2] For ancient beliefs regarding giants, see *Leopardi, Saggio*

In the midst of this appears an episode very comical but very instructive; for it shows that the attempt to shape the deductions of science to meet the exigencies of theology may mislead heterodoxy as absurdly as orthodoxy.

About the year 1760 news of the discovery of marine fossils in various elevated districts of Europe reached Voltaire. He, too, had a theologic system to support, though his system was opposed to that of the sacred books of the Hebrews. He feared that these new discoveries might be used to support the Mosaic accounts of the Deluge. All his wisdom and wit, therefore, were compacted into arguments to prove that the fossil fishes were remains of fishes intended for food, but spoiled and thrown away by travelers; that the fossil shells were accidentally dropped by Crusaders and pilgrims returning from the Holy Land; and that

sopra gli errori popolari, etc., chapter xv. For accounts of the views of Mazurier and Scheuchzer, see *Büchner, Man in Past, Present, and Future*, English translation, pp. 235, 236. For Increase Mather's views, see *Philosophical Transactions*, xxiv., 85. For similar fossils sent from New York to the Royal Society as remains of giants, see *Weld, History of the Royal Society*, vol. i., p. 421. For Father Torrubia and his *Gigantologia Española*, see *D'Archiac, Introduction à l'Étude de la Paléontologie stratiographique*, Paris, 1864, p. 202. For admirable summaries, see *Lyell, Principles of Geology*, London, 1867; *D'Archiac, Géologie et Paléontologie*, Paris, 1866; *Pictet, Traité de Paléontologie*, Paris, 1853; *Vezian, Prodrome de la Géologie*, Paris, 1863; *Haeckel, History of Creation*, New York, 1876, chapter iii.

sundry fossil bones found between Paris and
Étampes were parts of a skeleton belonging to the
cabinet of some ancient philosopher. Through
chapter after chapter, Voltaire, obeying the supposed necessities of his theology, fights desperate-
ly the growing results of the geologic investigations of his time.[1]

But far more widespread and disastrous was
the effort on the other side to show that the fossils
were caused by the Deluge of Noah.

No supposition was too violent to support a
theory which was considered vital to the Bible.
Sometimes it was claimed that the tail of a comet
had produced the Deluge. Sometimes, by a prosaic rendering of the expression regarding the
breaking up of "the fountains of the great deep,"
a theory was started that the earth contained a
great cistern, from which the waters came and to
which they retired. By taking sacred poetry as
prose, and by giving a literal interpretation of it,
Thomas Burnet, in his "Sacred Theory of the
Earth," Whiston, in his "Theory of the Deluge,"
and others like them, built up systems which bear
to real geology much the same relation that the
"Christian Topography" of Cosmas bears to real

[1] See *Voltaire, Dissertation sur les Changements arrivés dans notre Globe;* also, *Voltaire, Les Singularités de la Nature,* chapter xii., near close of vol. v. of the Didot edition of 1843; also,
Jevons, Principles of Science, vol. ii., p. 328.

geography. In vain were exhibited the absolute geological, zoölogical, astronomical proofs that no universal deluge, or deluge covering any great extent of the earth, had taken place within the last six thousand or sixty thousand years; in vain did Bishop Clayton declare, that the Deluge could not have taken place save in that district where Noah lived before the flood; in vain was it shown that, even if there had been a universal deluge, the fossils were not produced by it: the only answers were the citation of the text, "And all the high mountains which were under the whole heaven were covered," and denunciations of infidelity. In England, France, and Germany, belief that the fossils were produced by the Deluge of Noah was insisted upon as part of that faith essential to salvation.[1] It took a hundred and twenty years for the searchers of God's truth as revealed in Nature—such men as Buffon, Linnæus, Whitehurst, and Daubenton—to push their works under these mighty fabrics of error, and, by statements which could not be resisted, to explode them.

Strange as it may at first seem, the war on ge-

[1] For a candid summary of the proofs from geology, astronomy, and zoölogy, that the Noachian Deluge was not universally or widely extended, see *McClintock and Strong, Cyclopædia of Biblical Theology and Ecclesiastical Literature*, article *Deluge*. For general history, see *Lyell, D'Archiac*, and *Vezian*. For special cases showing bitterness of the conflict, see the *Rev. Mr. Davis's Life of Rev. Dr. Pye Smith, passim.*

ology was waged more fiercely in Protestant countries than in Catholic; the older Church had learned, by her earlier wretched mistakes, what dangers to her claim of infallibility lay in meddling with a growing science; in Italy, then entirely under papal control, little open opposition was made; and, of all countries, England furnished the most bitter opponents to geology at first, and the most active negotiators in patching up a truce on a basis of sham science afterward.[1]

You have noted already that there are, generally, two sorts of attack on a new science. First, there is the attack by pitting against science some great doctrine in theology. You saw this in astronomy, when Bellarmin and others insisted that the doctrine of the earth revolving about the sun is contrary to the doctrine of the incarnation. So now, against geology, it was urged that the scientific doctrine that the fossils represented animals which died before Adam, was contrary to the doctrine of Adam's fall, and that "death entered the world by sin."

Then, there is the attack by literal interpreta-

---

[1] For comparison between conduct of Italian and English ecclesiastics, as regards geology, see *Lyell, Principles of Geology*, tenth English ed., vol. i., p. 33. For a philosophical statement of reasons why the struggle was more bitter, and the attempt at deceptive compromises more absurd in England than elsewhere, see *Maury, L'Ancienne Académie des Sciences*, second edition, p. 152.

tion of texts, based upon the idea that the Bible is a compendium of history or a text-book of natural science, which serves a better purpose, generally, in rousing prejudices.

Toward the close of the last century, in England, the opponents of geology on Biblical grounds seemed likely to sweep all before them. Cramping our sacred volume within the rules of an historical compend, they showed the terrible dangers arising from the revelations of geology, which make the earth older than the six thousand years required by Archbishop Usher's interpretation of the Old Testament. Nor was this panic confined to ecclesiastics. Williams, a thoughtful layman, declared that such researches led to infidelity and atheism, and are "nothing less than to depose the Almighty Creator of the universe from his office." The poet Cowper, one of the mildest of men, was also roused by these dangers, and in his most elaborate poem wrote:

> "Some drill and bore
> The solid earth, and from the strata there
> Extract a register, by which we learn
> That he who made it, and revealed its date
> To Moses, was mistaken in its age!"

And difficult as it is to realize it now, within the memory of many of us the battle was still raging most fiercely in England, and both kinds of artillery usually brought against a new science were in full play, and filling the civilized world with their roar.

About thirty years ago, the Rev. J. Mellor Brown, the Rev. Henry Cole, and others, were hurling at all geologists alike, and especially at such Christian divines as Dr. Buckland and Dean Conybeare, and Pye Smith, and such religious scholars as Prof. Sedgwick, the epithets of "infidel," "impugner of the sacred record," and "assailant of the volume of God."[1]

Their favorite weapon was the charge that these men were "attacking the truth of God," forgetting that they were simply opposing the mistaken interpretations of Messrs. Brown, Cole, and others, like them, inadequately informed.

They declared geology "not a subject of lawful inquiry," denouncing it as "a dark art," as "dangerous and disreputable," as "a forbidden province," as "infernal artillery," and as "an awful evasion of the testimony of revelation."[2]

This attempt to scare men from the science having failed, various other means were taken. To say nothing about England, it is humiliating to human nature to remember the annoyances, and even trials, to which the pettiest and narrow-

---

[1] For these citations, see *Lyell, Principles of Geology*, introduction.

[2] See *Pye Smith, D. D., Geology and Scripture*, pp. 156, 157, 168, 169.

est of men subjected such Christian scholars in our own country as Benjamin Silliman and Edward Hitchcock and Louis Agassiz.

But it is a duty and a pleasure to state here that one great Christian scholar did honor to religion and to himself by standing up for the claims of science, despite all these clamors. That man was Nicholas Wiseman, better known afterward as Cardinal Wiseman. The conduct of this pillar of the Roman Catholic Church contrasts nobly with that of timid Protestants, who were filling England with shrieks and denunciations.[1]

And here let me note, that one of the prettiest skirmishes in this war was made in New England. Prof. Stuart, of Andover, justly honored as a Hebrew scholar, virtually declared that geology was becoming dangerous; that to speak of six periods of time for the creation was flying in the face of Scripture; that Genesis expressly speaks of six days, each made up of an evening and a morning, and not six periods of time.

To him replied a professor in Yale College, James Kingsley. In an article admirable for keen wit and kindly temper, he showed that Genesis speaks just as clearly of a solid firmament as of six ordinary days, and that if Prof. Stuart had

---

[1] *Wiseman, Twelve Lectures on the Connection between Science and Revealed Religion*, first American edition, New York, 1837.

got over one difficulty and accepted the Copernican theory, he might as well get over another and accept the revelations of geology. The encounter was quick and decisive, and the victory was with science and our own honored Yale.[1]

But perhaps the most singular attempt against geology was made by a fine specimen of the English Don—Dean Cockburn, of York—to *scold* its champions out of the field. Without, apparently, the simplest elementary knowledge of geology, he opened a battery of abuse. He gave it to the world at large, by pulpit and press; he even inflicted it upon leading statesmen by private letters.[2] From his pulpit in York minster, Mary Somerville was denounced coarsely, by name, for those studies in physical geography which have made her honored throughout the world.[3]

---

[1] See *Silliman's Journal*, vol. xxx., p. 114.

[2] Prof. Goldwin Smith informs me that the papers of Sir Robert Peel, yet unpublished, contain very curious specimens of these epistles.

[3] See *Personal Recollections of Mary Somerville*, Boston, 1874, pp. 139 and 375. Compare with any statement of his religious views that Dean Cockburn was able to make, the following from Mrs. Somerville: "Nothing has afforded me so convincing a proof of the Deity as these purely mental conceptions of numerical and mathematical science which have been, by slow degrees, vouchsafed to man—and are still granted in these latter times, by the differential calculus, now superseded by the higher algebra—all of which must have existed in that sublimely omniscient mind from eternity."—See *Personal Recollections*, pp. 140, 141.

But these weapons did not succeed. They were like Chinese gongs and dragon-lanterns against rifled cannon. Buckland, Pye Smith, Lyell, Silliman, Hitchcock, Murchison, Agassiz, Dana, and a host of noble champions besides, press on, and the battle for truth is won.

And was it won merely for men of science? The whole civilized world declares that it was won for religion—that thereby was infinitely increased the knowledge of the power and goodness of God.

POLITICAL ECONOMY.

From the many questions on which the supporters of right reason in Political and Social Science have only conquered conscientious opposition after centuries of war, I select the taking of interest on loans; in hardly any struggle has rigid adherence to the Bible as a scientific text-book been more prolonged or injurious.[1]

Certainly, if the criterion of truth, as regards any doctrine, be that it has been believed in the Church "always, everywhere, and by all," then on no point may a Christian of these days be more sure than that every savings-institution, every loan and trust company, every bank, every loan of

---

[1] For another great error of the Church in political economy, leading to injury to commerce, see *Lindsay, History of Merchant-Shipping*, London, 1874. vol. ii.

capital by an individual, every means by which accumulated capital has been lawfully lent, even at the most moderate interest, to make the masses of men workers rather than paupers, is based on deadly sin.

The fathers of the Christian Church received from the ancient world a strong prejudice against any taking of interest whatever; in Greece, Aristotle had condemned it; in Rome it was regarded during many generations as a crime.[1]

But far greater, in the early Church, was the influence of certain texts in the Old and New Testaments. Citations from Leviticus, Deuteronomy, the Psalms, Ezekiel, and St. Luke, were universally held to condemn all loans at interest.[2]

On these texts the doctrine and legislation of the universal Church, as regards interest for money, were based and developed. The fathers of the Eastern Church, and among them St. Basil, St. Chrysostom, and St. Gregory Nazianzen;

---

[1] See *Murray, History of Usury*, Philadelphia, 1866, p. 25; also, *Coquelin and Guillaumin, Dictionnaire de l'Économie Politique*, articles *Intérêt* and *Usure;* also, *Lecky, History of Rationalism in Europe*, vol. ii., chapter vi.; also, *Jeremy Bentham's Defence of Usury*, Letter X.; also, *Mr. D. S. Dickinson's Speech in the Senate of New York*, vol. i. of his collected writings. Of all the summaries, Lecky's is by far the best.

[2] The texts cited most frequently were Leviticus xxv. 36, 37; Deuteronomy xxiii. 19; Psalms xv. 5; Ezekiel xviii. 8 and 17; St. Luke vi. 35. See *Lecky;* also, *Dickinson's Speech*, as above.

the fathers of the Western Church, and among them Tertullian, St. Ambrose, St. Augustine, and St. Jerome, joined most earnestly in this condemnation. St. Chrysostom says: "What can be more unreasonable than to sow without land, without rain, without ploughs? All those who give themselves up to this damnable agriculture shall reap only tares. Let us cut off these monstrous births of gold and silver; let us stop this execrable fecundity." St. Jerome threw the argument into the form of a dilemma, which was used as a weapon against money-lenders for centuries.[1]

This entire agreement of the fathers of the Church led to the crystallization of the hostility to interest-bearing loans into numberless decrees of popes and councils, and kings and legislatures, throughout Christendom, during more than fifteen hundred years; and the canon law was shaped in accordance with these. In the ninth century, Alfred, in England, confiscated the estates of money-lenders, and denied them burial in consecrated ground; and similar decrees were made in other parts of Europe. In the twelfth century the Greek Church seems to have relaxed its strictness somewhat, but the Roman Church only grew more and more severe. St. Bernard, reviving religious

[1] See *Dictionnaire de l'Économie Politique*, articles *Intérêt* and *Usure* for these citations. For some doubtful reservations made by St. Augustine, see *Murray*.

earnestness in the Church, was especially strenuous in denouncing loans at interest; and, in 1179, the Third Council of the Lateran decreed that every impenitent money-lender should be excluded from the altar, from absolution in the hour of death, and from Christian burial!

In the thirteenth century this mistaken idea was still more firmly knit into the thought of the Church by St. Thomas Aquinas; hostility to loans at interest had been poured into his mind, not only from the Scriptures, but from Aristotle.

At the beginning of the fourteenth century the Council of Vienne, presided over by Pope Clement V., declared that, if any one "shall pertinaciously presume to affirm that the taking of interest for money is not a sin, we decree him to be a heretic fit for punishment."[1]

The economical and social results of this conscientious policy were exceedingly unfortunate. Money could only be loaned, in most countries, at the risk of incurring odium in this world and damnation in the next; hence there was but little capital and few lenders; hence came enormous rates of interest; thereby were commerce, manufactures, and general enterprise dwarfed, while pauperism flourished.

But even worse than this were the moral re-

---

[1] See citation of the Latin text in *Lecky*.

sults. For nations to do what they believe is evil, is only second in bad consequences to their doing what is really evil: all lending and borrowing, even for the most legitimate purposes and at the most reasonable rates, tended to debase the character of both borrower and lender.[1] And these moral evils took more definite shapes than might at first be thought possible. Sismondi, one of the most thoughtful of modern political philosophers and historians, declares that the prohibition of interest for the use of money in Continental Europe did very much to promote a passion for luxury and to discourage economy; the rich who were not engaged in business finding no easy way of employing their savings productively.[2]

These evils became so manifest, when trade began to revive throughout Europe in the fifteenth century, that most earnest efforts were made to induce the Church to change its position.

The first important effort of this kind was made by John Gerson. His general learning had made him Chancellor of the University of Paris; his sacred learning made him the leading theologian and orator at the Council of Constance; his piety led men to attribute to him "The Imitation

---

[1] For this moral effect, see *Montesquieu, Esprit des Lois*, lib. xxi., chap. xx.

[2] See citation in *Lecky.*

of Christ." Shaking off theological shackles, he declared: "Better is it to lend money at reasonable interest, and thus to give aid to the poor, than to see them reduced by poverty to steal, waste their goods, and sell, at a low price, their personal and real property."[1]

But this idea was at once suppressed by the Church—buried beneath citations from Scripture, the fathers, councils, popes, and the canon law. Even in the most active countries there seemed no hope. In England, under Henry VII., Cardinal Morton, the lord-chancellor, addressed Parliament, asking them to take into consideration loans of money at interest, and the result was a law which imposed on lenders at interest a fine of a hundred pounds, besides the annulment of the loan ; and, to show that there was an offence against religion involved, there was added a clause "reserving to the Church, notwithstanding this punishment, the correction of their souls according to the laws of the same."[2] Similar enactments were made by civil authority in various parts of Europe, and, as a climax, just as the trade and commerce and manufactures of the modern epoch had received an immense impulse from the great series of voyages of discovery, by such as Columbus, Vasco de Gama,

---

[1] See *Coquelin and Guillaumin*, article *Intérêt*.
[2] See *Craik's History of British Commerce*, chapter vi. The statute cited is 3 *Henry VII.*, chapter vi.

Magellan, and the Cabots, this barrier against enterprise was strengthened by a decree from Pope Leo X.[1]

But this mistaken policy was not confined to the older Church. The Reformed Church was led by Luther and several of his associates into the same line of thought and practice. Said Luther: "To exchange anything with any one and gain by the exchange, is not to do a charity, but to steal. Every usurer is a thief worthy of the gibbet. I call those usurers who lend money at five or six per cent."[2]

The English Reformers showed the same tendency. Under Henry VIII., the law of Henry VII. against taking interest had been modified; but the revival of religious feeling under Edward VI. caused, in 1552, the passage of the "Bill of Usury." In this it is said: "Forasmuch as usury is by the Word of God utterly prohibited, as a vice most odious and detestable, as in divers places of the Holy Scriptures it is evident to be seen, which thing by no godly teachings and persuasions can sink into the hearts of divers greedy, uncharitable, and covetous persons of this realm, nor yet by any terrible threatenings of God's wrath and ven-

---

[1] See *Lecky*.
[2] See citation from the *Tischreden*, in *Guillaumin and Coquelin*, article *Intérêt*.

geance," etc., etc., it is enacted that whosoever shall thereafter lend money "for any manner of usury, increase, lucre, gain, or interest, to be had, received, or hoped for," shall forfeit principal and interest, and suffer imprisonment and fine at the king's pleasure.[1]

But, most fortunately, it happened that Calvin turned in the right direction, and there was developed among Protestants the serviceable fiction that "usury" means *illegal* or *oppressive* interest. Under cover of this fiction commerce and trade revived rapidly in Protestant countries, though with occasional checks from exact interpreters of Scripture.

But, in the older Church, the more correct though less fortunate interpretation of the sacred texts relating to interest continued. When it was attempted in France, in the seventeenth century, to argue that "usury" means oppressive interest, the Theological Faculty of the Sorbonne declared that usury is the taking of any interest at all, no matter how little, and the eighteenth chapter of Ezekiel was cited to clinch this judgment.

Another attempt to ease the burden on industry and commerce was made by declaring that "usury means interest demanded not as matter of favor but as matter of right." This, too, was solemnly condemned by Pope Innocent XI.

[1] See *Craik's History of British Commerce*, chapter vi.

Again the army of right reason pressed forward, declaring that "usury is interest greater than the law allows." This, too, was condemned, and the declaration that "usury is interest on loans not for a fixed time" was condemned by Pope Alexander VII.

Still the attacking forces pressed on, and among them, in the seventeenth century, in France, was Richard Simon: he attempts to gloss over the strict interpretation of Scripture in this matter by an elaborate treatise: he is immediately confronted by Bossuet.

It seems hardly possible that one of the greatest intellects of a period so near us could have been so doubly deceived. Yet Bossuet, the glory of the French Church, one of the keenest and strongest of thinkers, not only mingled Scripture with astronomy, and opposed the Copernican theory, but also mingled Scripture with political economy, and denounced the lending of money at interest. He declared that the Scriptures, the councils of the Church from the beginning, the popes, the fathers, all interpreted the prohibition of "usury" to be a prohibition of any lending at interest, and Bossuet demonstrated this interpretation as the true one. Simon was put to confusion, and his book condemned.[1]

---

[1] For citation, as above, see *Lecky*. For further account, see *Œuvres de Bossuet*, edition of 1845, vol. xi., p. 330.

There was but too much reason for Bossuet's interpretation. The prohibition of this, one of the most simple and beneficial principles in political and economical science, was affirmed not only by the fathers, but by twenty-eight councils of the Church (six of them general councils), and by seventeen popes, to say nothing of innumerable doctors in theology and canon law.[1]

But about the middle of the eighteenth century the evil could be endured no longer—a way of escape *must* be found. The army opposed to the Church had become so formidable, that the Roman authorities saw that a concession must be made. In 1748 appeared Montesquieu's *Spirit of the Laws;* in it were concentrated twenty years' study and thought of a great thinker on the necessities of the world about him. In eighteen months it went through twenty-two editions, and it was translated into every civilized language; this work attacked, among other abuses, the position of the Church regarding interest for money.

The Church authorities had already taken the alarm. Benedict XIV. saw that the best thing for him—nay, the only thing—was a surrender under form of a compromise. In a brief he declared substantially that the law of the Church

---

[1] See citation from *Concina* in *Lecky;* also, acquiescence in this interpretation by *Mr. Dickinson, in Speech in Senate of New York,* above quoted.

was opposed to the taking of interest on loans; and then, after sundry non-committal and ambiguous statements, he hinted that there were possible exceptions to the rule.

Like the casuistry of Boscovich in using the Copernican theory for " convenience in argument," while acquiescing in its condemnation by the Church, this casuistry of Benedict broke the spell. Turgot, Adam Smith, Bentham, and their disciples, pressed on, and science won for mankind another great victory.

Yet in this case, as in others, insurrections against the sway of scientific truth appeared among some over-zealous religionists. When the Sorbonne, having retreated from its old position, armed itself with sundry new casuistries against those who held to its earlier decisions, provincial doctors in theology protested indignantly, making the old citations from the Scriptures, fathers, saints, doctors, popes, councils, and canonists. And even as late as 1830, when the Roman court, though declining to commit itself on the doctrine involved, decreed that confessors should no longer disquiet lenders of money at legal interest, the old weapons were again furbished and hurled by the Abbé Laborde, Vicar of the Metropolitan Archdiocese of Auch, and by the Abbé Dennavit, Professor of Theology at Lyons. Good Abbé Dennavit declared that he refused absolution to those who took interest, and to priests who pretend that the sanction of the civil law is sufficient.[1]

But the peace on this question is too profound to be disturbed by such outcries. The Torlonia family at Rome, to-day, with its palaces, chapels, intermarriages, affiliations, and papal favor, all won by lending money at interest, and by devotion to the Roman See, is a growth on ramparts long since surrendered and deserted.

INDUSTRIAL SCIENCES.

Did time permit, we might go over other battle-fields no less instructive than those we have seen. We might go over the battle-fields of Agricultural Progress, and note how, by a most curious perversion of a text of Scripture, many of the peasantry of Russia were prevented from raising and eating potatoes, and how in Scotland at the beginning of this century the use of fanning-mills for winnowing grain was denounced as contrary to the text "the wind bloweth where it listeth," etc., as leaguing with Satan, who is "prince of the powers of the air," and as sufficient cause for excommunication from the Scotch Church.[2]

---

[1] See *Réplique des douze Docteurs*, etc., cited by Guillaumin and Coquelin.

[2] *Burton, History of Scotland*, vol. viii., p. 511. See, also,

We might go over the battle-fields of Civil Engineering, and note how the introduction of railways into France was declared, by an Archbishop, to be an evidence of the divine displeasure against country innkeepers who set meat before their guests on fast-days, and now were punished by seeing travelers carried by their doors; and how railroad and telegraph were denounced from noted pulpits as "heralds of Antichrist." And then we might pass to Protestant England and recall the sermon of the Curate of Rotherhithe at the breaking in of the Thames Tunnel, so destructive to life and property, declaring that "it was but a just judgment upon the presumptuous aspirations of mortal man."[1]

VARIOUS SCIENCES.

We might go over the battle-fields of Ethnology and note how, a few years since, an honored American investigator, proposing in a learned society the discussion of the question between the

---

Mause Headrigg's views in Scott's *Old Mortality*, chapter vii. For the case of a person debarred from the communion for "raising the devil's wind" with a winnowing-machine, see *Works of Sir J. Y. Simpson*, vol. ii. Those doubting the authority or motives of Simpson may be reminded that he was, to the day of his death, one of the strictest adherents of Scotch orthodoxy.

[1] See *Journal of Sir I. Brunel*, for May 20, 1827, in *Life of I. K. Brunel*, p. 30.

origin of the human race from a single pair and from many pairs, was called to order and silenced as atheistic, by a Protestant divine whose memory is justly dear to thousands of us.[1]

Interesting would it be to look over the field of Meteorology—beginning with the conception, supposed to be scriptural, of angels opening and shutting "the windows of heaven" and letting out "the waters that be above the firmament" upon the earth—continuing through the battle of Fromundus and Bodin, down to the onslaught upon Lecky, in our own time, for drawing a logical and scientific conclusion from the doctrine that meteorology is obedient to laws.[2]

We might go over the battle-fields of Cartography and see how at one period, on account of expressions in Ezekiel, any map of the world which did not place Jerusalem in the centre, was looked on as impious.[3]

---

[1] This scene will be recalled, easily, by many leading ethnologists in America, and especially by Mr. E. G. Squier, formerly minister of the United States to Central America.

[2] The meteorological battle is hardly fought out yet. Many excellent men seem still to entertain views almost identical with those of over two thousand years ago, depicted in *The Clouds* of Aristophanes.

[3] These texts are Ezekiel v. 5 and xxxviii. 12. The progress of geographical knowledge, evidently, caused them to be softened down somewhat in our King James's version; but the first of them reads, in the Vulgate, "Ista est Hierusalem, in medio gen-

We might go over the battle-fields of Social Science in Protestant countries, and note the opposition of conscientious men to the taking of the census, in Sweden and in the United States, on account of the terms in which the numbering of Israel is spoken of in the Old Testament.[1]

And we might also see how, on similar grounds, religious scruples have been avowed against so beneficial a thing as Life Insurance.[2]

tium posui eam et in circuitu ejus terras;" and the second reads in the Vulgate "in medio terræ," and in the Septuagint ἐπὶ τὸν ὀμφαλὸν τῆς γῆς. That the literal centre of the earth was meant, see proof in St. Jerome, Commentar. in Ezekiel, lib. ii., and for general proof, see Leopardi, " Saggio sopra gli errori popolari degli antichi," pp. 207, 208. For an idea of orthodox geography in the middle ages, see *Wright's Essay on Archæology*, vol. ii., chapter "On the Map of the World in Hereford Cathedral." For an example of the depth to which this idea of Jerusalem as the centre had entered into the thinking of the great poet of the middle ages, see *Dante, Inferno, Canto xxxiv.*:

"E se' or sotto l'emisperio giunto,
 Ch' è opposito a quel, che la gran secca
 Coverchia, e sotto 'l cui colmo consunto
 Fu l'uom che nacque e visse senza pecca."

[1] See *Michaelis, Commentaries on the Laws of Moses*, 1874, vol. II., p. 3. The writer of the present article himself witnessed the reluctance of a very conscientious man to answer the questions of a census marshal, Mr. Lewis Hawley, of Syracuse, N. Y., and this reluctance was based upon the reasons assigned in II. Samuel chapter xxiv. 1, and I. Chronicles, chapter xxi. 1, for the numbering of the children of Israel.

[2] See *De Morgan, Paradoxes*, pp. 214–220.

SCIENTIFIC INSTRUCTION.

But an outline of this kind would be too meagre without some sketch of the warfare on instruction in science. Not without profit would it be to note more at length how instruction in the Copernican theory was kept out of the Church universities in every great Catholic country of Europe; how they concealed the discovery of the spots on the sun; how many of them excluded the Newtonian demonstrations; how, down to the present time, the two great universities of Protestant England and nearly all her intermediate colleges, under clerical supervision, have excluded the natural and physical sciences as far as possible; and how, from probably nine-tenths of the universities and colleges of the United States, the students are graduated with either no knowledge or with clerically emasculated knowledge of the most careful modern thought on the most important problems in the various sciences, in history, and in criticism.

From the dismissal of the scientific professors from the University of Salamanca by Ferdinand VII. of Spain, in the beginning of this century, down to sundry dealings with scientific men in our own land and time, we might study another interesting phase of the same warfare; but, passing all this, I shall simply present a few typical conflicts that have occurred within the last ten years.

During the years 1867 and 1868 the war which had been long smouldering in France, between the Church and the whole system of French advanced education, came to an outbreak. Toward the end of the last century, after the Church had held possession of advanced instruction in France for more than a thousand years, and had, so far as it was able, made experimental science contemptible; and after the Church authorities had deliberately resisted and wrecked Turgot's noble plans for the establishment of a system of public schools, the French nation decreed the establishment of the most thorough and complete system of the higher public instruction then known. It was kept under lay control, and became one of the great glories of France.

But, emboldened by the restoration of the Bourbons, the Church began to undermine the hated system, and in 1868 had made such progress that all was ready for an assault.

Foremost among the leaders of the besieging party was the Bishop of Orleans—Dupanloup—a man of much buzzing vigor. In various ways, and especially in an open letter, he had fought the "Materialism" of the School of Medicine at Paris, and especially were his attacks leveled at Professors Vulpian and Sec, and the Minister of Public Instruction, Duruy, a man of great merit, whose only crime was a quiet resistance to clerical control.[1]

In these writings, Bishop Dupanloup stigmatized Darwin, Huxley, Lyell, and others, as authors of "shameful theories," and made especial use of the recent phrase of a naturalist, that "it is more glorious to be a monkey perfected than an Adam degenerated."

The direct attack was made in the French Senate, and the storming party in that body was led by a venerable and conscientious prelate, Cardinal de Bonnechose.

It was charged by Archbishop de Bonnechose and his party, that the tendencies of the teachings of these professors were fatal to religion and morality. A heavy artillery of phrases was hurled, such as "sapping the foundations," etc., "breaking down the bulwarks," etc., etc., and, withal, a new missile was used with much effect, the epithet of "materialist." The result can be easily guessed; crowds came to the lecture-rooms of these professors, and the lecture-room of Prof. See, the chief offender, was crowded to suffocation.

A siege was begun in due form. A young physician was sent by the cardinal's party into the heterodox camp as a spy. Having heard one lecture of Prof. See, he returned with information

---

[1] For *Dupanloup, Lettre à un Cardinal,* see the *Revue de Thérapeutique,* 1868, p. 221.

that seemed to promise easy victory to the besieging party. He brought a terrible statement, one that seemed enough to overwhelm See, Vulpian, Duruy, and the whole hated system of public instruction in France.

Good Cardinal Bonnechose seized the tremendous weapon. Rising in his place in the Senate, he launched a most eloquent invective against the Minister of State who could protect such a fortress of impiety as the College of Medicine; and, as a climax, he asserted, on the evidence of his spy fresh from Prof. See's lecture-room, that the professor had declared, in his lecture of the day before, that so long as he had the honor to hold his professorship he would combat the false idea of the existence of the soul. The weapon seemed resistless, and the wound fatal; but M. Duruy rose and asked to be heard.

His statement was simply that he held in his hand documentary proofs that Prof. See never made such a declaration. He held the notes used by Prof. See in his lecture. Prof. See, it appeared, belonged to a school in medical science which combated the idea of an art in medicine. The inflamed imagination of the cardinal's too eager emissary had, as the lecture notes proved, led him into a sad mistake as to words and thoughts, and had exhibited Prof. See as treating a theological when he was discussing a purely scientific question. Of the existence of the soul the professor had said nothing.

The forces of the enemy were immediately turned; they retreated in confusion, amid the laughter of all France; and a quiet, dignified statement as to the rights of scientific instructors by Wurtz, the dean of the Faculty, completed their discomfiture. Thus a well-meant attempt to check what was feared might be dangerous in science simply ended in bringing ridicule on religion, and thrusting still deeper into the minds of thousands of men that most mistaken of all mistaken ideas—the conviction that religion and science are enemies.[1]

But justice forbids our raising an outcry against Roman Catholicism alone for this. In 1864 a number of excellent men in England drew up a declaration to be signed by students in the natural sciences, expressing "sincere regret that researches into scientific truth are perverted by some in our time into occasion for casting doubt upon the truth and authenticity of the Holy Scriptures."

---

[1] For general account of the Vulpian and See matter, see *Revue des Deux Mondes*, 31 Mai, 1868. *Chronique de la Quinzaine*, pp. 763–765. As to the result on popular thought, may be noted the following comment on the affair by the *Revue*, which is as free as possible from anything like rabid anti-ecclesiastical ideas: "*Elle a été vraiment curieuse, instructive, assez triste et même un peu amusante.*" For Wurtz's statement, see *Revue de Thérapeutique* for 1868, p. 803.

Nine-tenths of the leading scientific men of England refused to sign it. Nor was this the worst. Sir John Herschel, Sir John Bowring, and Sir W. R. Hamilton, administered, through the press, castigations which roused general indignation against the proposers of the circular, and Prof. De Morgan, by a parody, covered memorial and memorialists with ridicule. It was the old mistake, and the old result followed in the minds of multitudes of thoughtful young men.[1]

And in yet another Protestant country this same wretched mistake was made. In 1868, several excellent churchmen in Prussia thought it their duty to meet for the denunciation of "science falsely so called." Two results followed: Upon the great majority of these really self-sacrificing men—whose first utterances showed crass ignorance of the theories they attacked—there came quiet and widespread contempt; upon Pastor Knak, who stood forth and proclaimed views of the universe which he thought Scriptural, but which most schoolboys knew to be childish, came a burst of good-natured derision from every quarter of the German nation.[2]

Warfare of this sort against Science seems petty indeed; but it is to be guarded against in

[1] *De Morgan, Paradoxes*, pp. 421–428; also, *Daubeny's Essays*.
[2] See the Berlin newspapers for the summer of 1868, especially *Kladderadatsch*.

Protestant countries not less than in Catholic; it breaks out in America not less than in Europe. I might exhibit many proofs of this. Do conscientious Roman bishops in France labor to keep all advanced scientific instruction under their own control—in their own universities and colleges; so do very many not less conscientious Protestant clergymen in our own country insist that advanced education in science and literature shall be kept under control of their own sectarian universities and colleges, wretchedly one-sided in their development, and miserably inadequate in their equipment: did a leading Spanish university, until a recent period, exclude professors holding the Newtonian theory; so does a leading American college exclude professors holding the Darwinian theory: have Catholic colleges in Italy rejected excellent candidates for professorships on account of "unsafe" views regarding the Immaculate Conception; so are Protestant colleges in America every day rejecting excellent candidates on account of "unsafe" views regarding the Apostolic Succession, or the Incarnation, or Baptism, or the Perseverance of the Saints.

And how has all this system resulted? In the older nations, by natural reaction, these colleges, under strict ecclesiastical control, have sent forth the most bitter enemies the Christian Church has ever known—of whom Voltaire and Renan and

Saint-Beuve are types; and there are many signs that the same causes are producing the same result in our own country.

I might allude to another battle-field in our own land and time. I might show how an attempt to meet the great want, in the State of New York, of an institution providing scientific instruction, has been met with loud outcries from many excellent men, who fear injury thereby to religion. I might picture to you the strategy which has been used to keep earnest young men from an institution which, it is declared, cannot be Christian because it is not sectarian. I might lay before you wonderful lines of argument which have been made to show the dangerous tendencies of a plan which gives to scientific studies the same weight as to classical studies, and which lays no less stress on modern history and literature than on ancient history and literature.

I might show how it has been denounced by the friends and agents of denominational colleges and in many sectarian journals; how the most preposterous charges have been made and believed by good men; how the epithets of "godless," "infidel," "irreligious," "unreligious," "atheistic," have been hurled against a body of Christian trustees, professors, and students, and with little practical result save arousing a suspicion in the minds of large bodies of thoughtful young men, that the churches dread scientific studies untrammeled by sectarianism.

SUMMARY.

You have now gone over the greater struggles in the long war between Ecclesiasticism and Science, and have glanced at the lesser fields. You have seen the conflicts in Physical Geography, as to the form of the earth; in Astronomy, as to the place of the earth in the universe, and the evolution of stellar systems in accordance with law; in Chemistry and Physics; in Anatomy and Medicine; in Geology; in Meteorology; in Cartography; in the Industrial and Agricultural Sciences; in Political Economy and Social Science; and in Scientific Instruction; and each of these, when fully presented, has shown the following results:

First. In every case, whether the war has been long or short, forcible or feeble, Science has at last gained the victory.

Secondly. In every case, interference with Science, in the supposed interest of religion, has brought dire evils on both.

Thirdly. In every case, while this interference, during its continuance, has tended to divorce religion from the most vigorous thinking of the world, and to make it odious to multitudes of the most earnest thinkers; the triumph of Science has led its former conscientious enemies to make new interpretations and lasting adjustments, which have proved a blessing to religion, ennobling its conceptions and bettering its methods.

And in addition to these points there should be brought out distinctly a *corollary*, which is, that science must be studied by its own means and to its own ends, unmixed with the means and unbiased by the motives of investigators in other fields, and uncontrolled by consciences unenlightened by itself.

The very finger of the Almighty seems to have written the proofs of this truth on human history. No one can gainsay it. It is decisive, for it is this: *There has never been a scientific theory framed from the use of Scriptural texts, wholly or partially, which has been made to stand.* Such attempts have only subjected their authors to derision, and Christianity to suspicion. From Cosmas finding his plan of the universe in the Jewish tabernacle, to Increase Mather sending mastodon's bones to England as the remains of giants mentioned in Scripture; from Bellarmin declaring that the sun cannot be the centre of the universe, because such an idea "vitiates the whole Scriptural plan of salvation," to a recent writer declaring that an evolution theory cannot be true, because St. Paul says that "all flesh is not the same flesh," the result has always been the same.[1]

[1] In the *Church Journal*, New York, May 28, 1874, a reviewer,

SUMMARY.

Such facts show that scientific hypothesis will be established or refuted by scientific men and scientific methods alone, and that no conscientious citation of texts, or outcries as to consequences of scientific truths, from any other quarter, can do any thing save retard truth and cause needless anxiety.[1]

praising Rev. Dr. Hodge's book against Darwinism, says: "Darwinism—whether Darwin knows it or not; whether the clergy, who are half prepared to accept it in blind fright as 'science,' know it or not—is a denial of every article of the Christian faith. It is supreme folly to talk as some do about accommodating Christianity to Darwinism. Either those who so talk do not understand Christianity, or they do not understand Darwinism. If we have all, men and monkeys, women and baboons, oysters and eagles, all 'developed' from an original monad and germ, then St. Paul's grand deliverance—' All flesh is not the same flesh. There is one kind of flesh of men, another of beasts, another of fishes, and another of birds. There are bodies celestial and bodies terrestrial '—may be still very grand in our funeral-service, but very untrue to fact." This is the same dangerous line of argument which Caccini indulged in in Galileo's time. Dangerous, for suppose "Darwinism" be .proved true! For a soothing potion by a skillful hand, see *Whewell* on the consistency of evolution doctrines with teleological ideas; also, *Rev. Samuel Houghton, F. R. S., Principles of Animal Mechanics*, London, 1873, preface, and page 156, for some interesting ideas on teleological evolution.

[1] For some excellent remarks on the futility of such attempts and outcries, see the *Rev. Dr. Deems, in* POPULAR SCIENCE MONTHLY for February, 1876. To all who are inclined to draw scientific conclusions from Biblical texts, may be commended the advice of a good old German divine of the Reformation period: "Seeking the milk of the Word, do not press the teats of Holy Writ too hard."

Such facts show, too, that the sacred books of the world were not given for any such purpose as that to which so many men have endeavored to wrest them—the purpose served by compends of history and text-books of science.

Is skepticism feared? All history shows that the only skepticism which does permanent harm is skepticism as to the value and safety of truth as truth. No skepticism has proved so corrosive to religion, none so cancerous in the human brain and heart.

Is faith cherished? All history shows that the first article of a saving faith, for any land or time, is faith that there is a Power in this universe strong enough to make truth-seeking safe, and good enough to make truth-telling useful.

May we not, then, hope that the greatest and best men in the Church—the men standing at centres of thought—will insist with power, more and more, that religion be no longer tied to so injurious a policy as that which this warfare reveals; that searchers for truth, whether in theology or natural science, work on as friends, sure that, no matter how much at variance they may at times seem to be, the truths they reach shall finally be fused into each other? The dominant religious conceptions of the world will doubtless be greatly modified by science in the future, as they have been in the past; and the part of any wisely religious person, at any centre of influence, is to see that, in his generation, this readjustment of religion to science be made as quietly and speedily as possible.

No one needs fear the result. No matter whether Science shall complete her demonstration that man has been on the earth not merely six thousand years, or six millions of years; no matter whether she reveals new ideas of the Creator or startling relations between his creatures; no matter how many more gyves and clamps upon the spirit of Christianity she destroys: the result, when fully thought out, will serve and strengthen religion not less than science.[1]

What science can do for the world is shown, not by those who have labored to concoct palatable mixtures of theology and science—men like

[1] In an eloquent sermon, preached in March, 1874, Bishop Cummins said, in substance: "The Church has no fear of Science; the persecution of Galileo was entirely unwarrantable; but Christians should resist to the last Darwinism; for that is evidently contrary to Scripture." The bishop forgets that Galileo's doctrine seemed to such colossal minds as Bellarmin, and Luther, and Bossuet, "evidently contrary to Scripture." Far more logical, modest, sagacious, and full of faith, is the attitude taken by his former associate, Dr. John Cotton Smith: "For geology, physiology, and historical criticism have threatened or destroyed only particular forms of religious opinion, while they have set the spirit of religion free to keep pace with the larger generalizations of modern knowledge."—*Picton, The Mystery of Matter*, London, 1873, p. 72.

Cosmas, and Torrubia, and Burnet, and Whiston—but by men who have fought the good fight of faith in truth for truth's sake—men like Roger Bacon, and Vesalius, and Palissy, and Galileo.

What Christianity can do for the world is shown, not by men who have stood on the high places screaming in wrath at the advance of science; not by men who have retreated in terror into the sacred caves and refused to look out upon the universe as it is; but by men who have preached and practised the righteousness of the prophets, and the aspirations of the Psalmist, and the blessed Sermon on the Mount, and "the first great commandment, and the second which is like unto it," and St. James's definition of "pure religion and undefiled."

It is shown in the Roman Church, not by Tostatus and Bellarmin, but by St. Carlo Borromeo, and St. Vincent de Paul, and Fénelon, and Eugénie de Guérin; in the Anglican Church, not by Dean Cockburn, but by Howard, and Jenner, and Wilberforce, and Florence Nightingale; in the German Church, not by Pastor Knak, but by Pastor Fliedner; in the American Church, not by the Mathers, but by such as Bishop Whatcoat, and Channing, and Muhlenberg, and Father De Smet, and Samuel May, and Harriet Stowe.

Let the warfare of Science, then, be changed. Let it be a warfare in which Religion and Science shall stand together as allies, not against each other as enemies. Let the fight be for truth of every kind against falsehood of every kind; for justice against injustice; for right against wrong; for the living kernel of religion rather than the dead and dried husks of sect and dogma; and the great powers, whose warfare has brought so many sufferings, shall at last join in ministering through earth God's richest blessings.

THE END.

SCIENTIFIC PUBLICATIONS.

Sight:

An Exposition of the Principles of Monocular and Binocular Vision. By JOSEPH LE CONTE, LL. D., author of "Elements of Geology," "Religion and Science," and Professor of Geology and Natural History in the University of California. With numerous Illustrations. 12mo. Cloth, $1.50.

"It is pleasant to find an American book which can rank with the very best of foreign works on this subject. Professor Le Conte has long been known as an original investigator in this department; all that he gives us is treated with a master-hand."—*The Nation.*

Animal Life,

As affected by the Natural Conditions of Existence. By KARL SEMPER, Professor of the University of Würzburg. With Two Maps and One Hundred and Six Woodcuts, and Index. 12mo. Cloth, $2.00.

"It appears to me that, of all the properties of the animal organism, Variability is that which may first and most easily be traced by exact investigation to its efficient causes; and as it is beyond a doubt the subject around which, at the present moment, the strife of opinions is most violent, it is that which will be most likely to repay the trouble of closer research. I have endeavored to facilitate this task so far as in me lies."—*From the Preface.*

The Atomic Theory.

By AD. WURTZ, Membre de l'Institut; Doyen Honoraire de la Faculté de Médecine; Professeur à la Faculté des Sciences de Paris. Translated by E. CLEMINSHAW, M. A., F. C. S., F. I. C., Assistant Master at Sherborne School. 12mo. Cloth, $1.50.

"There was need for a book like this, which discusses the atomic theory both in its historic evolution and in its present form. And perhaps no man of this age could have been selected so able to perform the task in a masterly way as the illustrious French chemist, Adolph Wurtz. It is impossible to convey to the reader, in a notice like this, any adequate idea of the scope, lucid instructiveness, and scientific interest of Professor Wurtz's book. The modern problems of chemistry, which are commonly so obscure from imperfect exposition, are here made wonderfully clear and attractive."—*The Popular Science Monthly.*

Education as a Science.

By ALEXANDER BAIN, LL. D. 12mo. Cloth, $1.75.

"This work must be pronounced the most remarkable discussion of educational problems which has been published in our day. It should be in the hands of every school-teacher and friend of education throughout the land."—*New York Sun.*

New York: D. APPLETON & CO., 1, 3, & 5 Bond Street.

SCIENTIFIC PUBLICATIONS.

Suicide:

An Essay in Comparative Moral Statistics. By HENRY MORSELLI, Professor of Psychological Medicine in the Royal University, Turin. 12mo. Cloth, $1.75.

"A most valuable contribution to English literature touching a theme most distressing in the act and terrible in its consequences, yet to this hour but very imperfectly studied or understood."—*Philadelphia Times.*

Volcanoes:

What they Are and what they Teach. By J. W. JUDD, Professor of Geology in the Royal School of Mines (London). With Ninety-six Illustrations. 12mo. Cloth, $2.00.

"In no field has modern research been more fruitful than in that of which Professor Judd gives a popular account in the present volume. The great lines of dynamical, geological, and meteorological inquiry converge upon the grand problem of the interior constitution of the earth, and the vast influence of subterranean agencies.... His book is very far from being a mere dry description of volcanoes and their eruptions; it is rather a presentation of the terrestrial facts and laws with which volcanic phenomena are associated."—*Popular Science Monthly.*

The Sun:

By C. A. YOUNG, Ph. D., LL. D., Professor of Astronomy in the College of New Jersey. With numerous Illustrations. Third edition, revised, with Supplementary Note. 12mo. Cloth, $2.00.

The "Supplementary Note" gives important developments in solar astronomy since the publication of the second edition in 1882.

"There is no rhetoric in his book; he trusts the grandeur of his theme to kindle interest and impress the feelings. His statements are plain, direct, clear, and condensed, though ample enough for his purpose, and the substance of what is generally wanted will be found accurately given in his pages."—*Popular Science Monthly.*

Illusions:

A Psychological Study. By JAMES SULLY, author of "Sensation and Intuition," etc. 12mo. Cloth, $1.50.

"An interesting contribution by Mr. James Sully to the study of mental pathology. The author's field of inquiry covers all the phenomena of illusion observed in sense-perception, in the introspection of the mind's own feelings, in the reading of others' feelings, in memory, and in belief. The author's conclusions are often illustrated by concrete example or anecdote, and his general treatment of the subject, while essentially scientific, is sufficiently clear and animated to attract the general reader."—*New York Sun.*

New York: D. APPLETON & CO., 1, 8, & 5 Bond Street.

SCIENTIFIC PUBLICATIONS.

The Brain and its Functions.

By J. Luys, Physician to the Hospice de la Salpêtrière. With Illustrations. 12mo. Cloth, $1.50.

"No living physiologist is better entitled to speak with authority upon the structure and functions of the brain than Dr. Luys. His studies on the anatomy of the nervous system are acknowledged to be the fullest and most systematic ever undertaken. Dr. Luys supports his conclusions not only by his own anatomical researches, but also by many functional observations of various other physiologists, including of course Professor Ferrier's now classical experiments."—*St. James's Gazette.*

The Concepts and Theories of Modern Physics.

By J. B. Stallo. 12mo. Cloth, $1.75.

"Judge Stallo's work is an inquiry into the validity of those mechanical conceptions of the universe which are now held as fundamental in physical science. He takes up the leading modern doctrines which are based upon this mechanical conception, such as the atomic constitution of matter, the kinetic theory of gases, the conservation of energy, the nebular hypothesis, and other views, to find how much stands upon solid empirical ground, and how much rests upon metaphysical speculation. Since the appearance of Dr. Draper's 'Religion and Science,' no book has been published in the country calculated to make so deep an impression on thoughtful and educated readers as this volume.... The range and minuteness of the author's learning, the acuteness of his reasoning, and the singular precision and clearness of his style, are qualities which very seldom have been jointly exhibited in a scientific treatise."—*New York Sun.*

The Formation of Vegetable Mould,

Through the Action of Worms, with Observations on their Habits. By Charles Darwin, LL. D., F. R. S., author of "On the Origin of Species," etc., etc. With Illustrations. 12mo. Cloth, $1.50.

"Mr. Darwin's little volume on the habits and instincts of earthworms is no less marked than the earlier or more elaborate efforts of his genius by freshness of observation, unfailing power of interpreting and correlating facts, and logical vigor in generalizing upon them. The main purpose of the work is to point out the share which worms have taken in the formation of the layer of vegetable mould which covers the whole surface of the land in every moderately humid country. All lovers of nature will unite in thanking Mr. Darwin for the new and interesting light he has thrown upon a subject so long overlooked, yet so full of interest and instruction, as the structure and the labors of the earth-worm."—*Saturday Review.*

New York: D. APPLETON & CO., 1, 3, & 5 Bond Street.

SCIENTIFIC PUBLICATIONS.

Ants, Bees, and Wasps.

A Record of Observations on the Habits of the Social Hymenoptera. By Sir JOHN LUBBOCK, Bart., M. P., F. R. S., etc., author of "Origin of Civilization, and the Primitive Condition of Man," etc., etc. With Colored Plates. 12mo, cloth, $2.00.

"This volume contains the record of various experiments made with ants, bees, and wasps during the last ten years, with a view to test their mental condition and powers of sense. The principal point in which Sir John's mode of experiment differs from those of Huber, Forel, McCook, and others, is that he has carefully watched and marked particular insects, and has had their nests under observation for long periods—one of his ants' nests having been under constant inspection ever since 1874. His observations are made principally upon ants because they show more power and flexibility of mind; and the value of his studies is that they belong to the department of original research."

Diseases of Memory.

An Essay in the Positive Psychology. By TH. RIBOT, author of "Heredity," etc. Translated from the French by WILLIAM HUNTINGTON SMITH. 12mo, cloth, $1.50.

"M. Ribot reduces diseases of memory to law, and his treatise is of extraordinary interest."—*Philadelphia Press.*

"Not merely to scientific, but to all thinking men, this volume will prove intensely interesting."—*New York Observer.*

"M. Ribot has bestowed the most painstaking attention upon his theme, and numerous examples of the conditions considered greatly increase the value and interest of the volume."—*Philadelphia North American.*

Myth and Science.

By TITO VIGNOLI. 12mo, cloth, price, $1.50.

"His book is ingenious; . . . his theory of how science gradually differentiated from and conquered myth is extremely well wrought out, and is probably in essentials correct."—*Saturday Review.*

"The book is a strong one, and far more interesting to the general reader than its title would indicate. The learning, the acuteness, the strong reasoning power, and the scientific spirit of the author, command admiration."—*New York Christian Advocate.*

"An attempt made, with much ability and no small measure of success, to trace the origin and development of the myth. The author has pursued his inquiry with much patience and ingenuity, and has produced a very readable and luminous treatise."—*Philadelphia North American.*

New York: D. APPLETON & CO., 1, 3, & 5 Bond Street.

SCIENTIFIC PUBLICATIONS.

Man before Metals.

By N. JOLY, Professor at the Science Faculty of Toulouse; Correspondent of the Institute. With 148 Illustrations. 12mo, cloth, $1.75.

"The discussion of man's origin and early history, by Professor De Quatrefages, formed one of the most useful volumes in the 'International Scientific Series,' and the same collection is now further enriched by a popular treatise on paleontology, by M. N. Joly, Professor in the University of Toulouse. The title of the book, 'Man before Metals,' indicates the limitations of the writer's theme. His object is to bring together the numerous proofs, collected by modern research, of the great age of the human race, and to show us what man was, in respect of customs, industries, and moral or religious ideas, before the use of metals was known to him."—*New York Sun.*

"An interesting, not to say fascinating volume."—*New York Churchman.*

Animal Intelligence.

By GEORGE J. ROMANES, F. R. S., Zoölogical Secretary of the Linnæan Society, etc. 12mo, cloth, $1.75.

"Unless we are greatly mistaken, Mr. Romanes's work will take its place as one of the most attractive volumes of the 'International Scientific Series.' Some persons may, indeed, be disposed to say that it is too attractive, that it feeds the popular taste for the curious and marvelous without supplying any commensurate discipline in exact scientific reflection; but the author has, we think, fully justified himself in his modest preface. The result is the appearance of a collection of facts which will be a real boon to the student of Comparative Psychology, for this is the first attempt to present systematically well-assured observations on the mental life of animals."—*Saturday Review.*

The Science of Politics.

By SHELDON AMOS, M. A., author of "The Science of Law," etc. 12mo, cloth, $1.75.

"The author traces the subject from Plato and Aristotle in Greece, and Cicero in Rome, to the modern schools in the English field, not slighting the teachings of the American Revolution or the lessons of the French Revolution of 1793. Forms of government, political terms, the relation of law, written and unwritten, to the subject, a codification from Justinian to Napoleon in France and Field in America, are treated as parts of the subject in hand. Necessarily the subjects of executive and legislative authority, police, liquor, and land laws are considered, and the question ever growing in importance in all countries, the relations of corporations to the state."—*New York Observer.*

New York: D. APPLETON & CO., 1, 3, & 5 Bond Street.

D. APPLETON & CO.'S PUBLICATIONS.

DARWINISM STATED BY DARWIN HIMSELF: Characteristic Passages from the Writings of Charles Darwin. Selected and arranged by Professor NATHAN SHEPPARD. 12mo, cloth, 360 pages, $1.50.

"Mr. Sheppard must be credited with exemplifying the spirit of impartial truth-seeking which inspired Darwin himself. From these condensed results of the hard labor of selection, excision, and arrangement applied to more than a dozen volumes, it is impossible to draw any inference respecting the philosophical opinions of the compiler. With the exception of a brief preface there is not a word of comment, nor is there the faintest indication of an attempt to infuse into Darwin's text a meaning not patent there, by unwarranted sub-titles or head-lines, by shrewd omission, unfair emphasis, or artful collocation. Mr. Sheppard has nowhere swerved from his purpose of showing in a clear, connected, and very compendious form, not what Darwin may have meant or has been charged with meaning, but what he actually said."—*The Sun.*

MENTAL EVOLUTION IN ANIMALS. By GEORGE J. ROMANES, author of "Animal Intelligence." With a Posthumous Essay on Instinct, by CHARLES DARWIN. 12mo, cloth, $2.00.

"The author confines himself to the psychology of the subject. Not only are his own views Darwinian, but he has incorporated in his work considerable citations from Darwin's unpublished manuscripts, and he has appended a Posthumous Essay on Instinct by Mr. Darwin."—*Boston Journal.*

"A curious but richly suggestive volume."—*New York Herald.*

PRACTICAL ESSAYS. By ALEXANDER BAIN, LL. D., author of "Mind and Body," "Education as a Science," etc. 12mo, cloth, $1.50.

"The present volume is in part a reprint of articles contributed to reviews. The principal bond of union among them is their practical character. ... That there is a certain amount of novelty in the various suggestions here embodied will be admitted on the most cursory perusal."—*From the Preface.*

THE ESSENTIALS OF ANATOMY, PHYSIOLOGY, AND HYGIENE. By ROGER S. TRACY, M. D., Health Inspector of the New York Board of Health; author of "Hand-Book of Sanitary Information for Householders," etc. (Forming a volume of Appletons' Science Text-Books.) 12mo, cloth, $1.25.

"Dr. Tracy states in his preface that his aim has been 'to compress within the narrowest space such a clear and intelligible account of the structures, activities, and care of the human system as is essential for the purposes of general education.' And he has so far succeeded as to make his manual one of the most popularly interesting and useful text-books of its kind. ... The book is excellently arranged, the illustrations are admirable."—*Boston Daily Advertiser.*

New York: D. APPLETON & CO., 1, 3, & 5 Bond Street.

D. APPLETON & CO.'S PUBLICATIONS.

HISTORY OF THE WORLD, from the Earliest Records to the Fall of the Western Empire. By PHILIP SMITH, B.A. New edition. 3 vols. 8vo. Vellum cloth, gilt top, $6.00; half calf, $13.50.

"These volumes embody the results of many years of arduous and conscientious study. The work is fully entitled to be called the ablest and most satisfactory book on the subject written in our language. The author's methods are dignified and judicious, and he has availed himself of all the recent light thrown by philological research on the annals of the East."—*Dr. C. K. Adams's Manual of Historical Literature.*

HISTORY OF HERODOTUS. An English Version, edited, with Copious Notes and Appendices, by GEORGE RAWLINSON, M.A. With Maps and Illustrations. In four volumes, 8vo. Vellum cloth, $8.00; half calf, $18.00.

"This must be considered as by far the most valuable version of the works of 'The Father of History.' The history of Herodotus was probably not written until near the end of his life; it is certain that he had been collecting materials for it during many years. There was scarcely a city of importance in Greece, Asia Minor, Syria, Persia, Arabia, or Egypt, that he had not visited and studied; and almost every page of his work contains results of his personal inquiries and observations. Many things laughed at for centuries as impossible are now found to have been described in strict accordance with truth."—*Dr. C. K. Adams's Manual of Historical Literature.*

A GENERAL HISTORY OF GREECE, from the Earliest Period to the Death of Alexander the Great. With a Sketch of the Subsequent History to the Present Time. By G. W. Cox. 12mo. Cloth, $1.50.

"One of the best of the smaller histories of Greece."—*Dr. C. K. Adams's Manual of Historical Literature.*

A HISTORY OF GREECE. From the Earliest Times to the Present. By T. T. TIMAYENIS. With Maps and Illustrations. 2 vols. 12mo. Cloth, $2.50.

"The peculiar feature of the present work is that it is founded on Hellenic sources. I have not hesitated to follow the Father of History in portraying the heroism and the sacrifices of the Hellenes in their first war for independence, nor, in delineating the character of that epoch, to form my judgment largely from the records he has left us."—*Extract from Preface.*

GREECE IN THE TIMES OF HOMER. An Account of the Life, Customs, and Habits of the Greeks during the Homeric Period. By T. T. TIMAYENIS. 16mo. Cloth, $1.50.

"In the preparation of the present volume I have conscientiously examined nearly every book—Greek, German, French, or English—written on Homer. But my great teacher and guide has been Homer himself."—*From the Preface.*

New York: D. APPLETON & CO., 1, 3, & 5 Bond Street.

www.ingramcontent.com/pod-product-compliance
Lightning Source LLC
Chambersburg PA
CBHW030316170426
43202CB00009B/1018